CW01657639

Tube Trivia

An A–Z of fascinating facts
about the London Underground

Andrew Emmerson

CAPITAL HISTORY

ISBN 978-185414-479-9

First published 2013
This edition 2023
Reprinted 2025

Published by
Capital History
www.capitalhistory.co.uk

Printed in the EU

Photo Credits

Antony Badsey-Ellis 43

Capital Transport 7, 10, 20, 22, 24, 36, 38, 40, 41, 42, 50, 54, 60, 62, 63, 71, 76, 79, 82, 88, 92

London Underground Ltd 18

Hulton Getty 53

Ken Garland 48

London Transport Museum 47, 64, 68, 80

Plessey Telecommunications 29

Press Association 9, 11, 23, 67

Kim Rennie 15, 74, 83, 85, 89

Contents

Introduction

So you think you know the Tube? Many people profess they do but few will fail to discover something novel in this substantial compilation of fascinating facts and figures. Determined not to repeat the same selection as found in other books and websites, I have tried to focus on the more unusual and quirky aspects of the Underground's geography, history and operations. It would be wrong, however, to ignore the more obvious subjects that intrigue people, so this book will certainly stand you in good stead if you are revising for the next pub quiz on London subjects. It will also make ideal reading matter for keeping you occupied when you next attempt the Tube Challenge to visit all the stations on the London Underground network in the fastest time possible!

Every entry in this book has been scrutinised by a panel of experts who include current and past London Underground staff. The opportunity has also been taken to debunk several hoary old myths previously taken as entirely factual. The book's keywords and A to Z format should make it easy to locate a particular piece of information but the book can equally enjoyed by dipping into it randomly. Perhaps you will find yourself hooked into reading the whole text from cover to cover.

Thanks are due to Mike Horne, Antony Badsey-Ellis and the London Underground press office for assistance with some of the information.

Andrew Emmerson

A

Acton Town was the first Underground station to have a one-man operated train running from it (in fact, being a single carriage, it was not strictly speaking a train, but was referred to as such). It operated in this form on a short shuttle service to South Acton and ran between 1932 and 1959 when this branch line was closed.

Air conditioning — a 75 year saga
The first experiments to reduce the stuffiness of carriages in hot and humid weather took place in late 1934 when a single coach on the Northern Line was fitted with Frigidaire air conditioning equipment under the seating and below the floor. The existing windows and vents were sealed, including the drop windows in the communicating doors and the side windows in the coach were upgraded with double glazing. Cool air was blown into the coach via a cowl running along the centre of the ceiling. The modified coach ran until April 1935 but the experiment was not successful and the coach was converted back to its original condition by the end of that year. Another 75 years were to pass before air conditioning was perfected for Underground trains. The lines on which air conditioning is being installed today are ones where the technology is mature but the need for it is hardly compelling. The technical challenge and the real benefits in passenger comfort both relate to deep tubes, for which there is not yet a solution to removal of heat from train interiors without transferring it to the platforms.

Aldwych station (Strand until 1915) closed to passenger services in 1994 but lives on as a venue for filming and occasional public visits. Its original station frontages are both still intact. At a number of points in its history, the short branch of the Piccadilly Line it served was unsuccessfully proposed for extension to Waterloo.

Angel station has the longest escalators *(right)* anywhere in London (three of 27.4 metres rise). They were brought into use in 1992 when the station was completely rebuilt. It also has an extra wide southbound platform built on what was previously an island platform here serving trains in both directions. A similar wide platform exists at Euston (southbound City branch).

Arnos Grove station, built in 1932, is based on the design of the main public library in Stockholm, built in 1928. The station is widely regarded as one of the finest works by the architect Charles Holden. The Underground's commercial manager, Frank Pick, and Holden, whose work first appeared in the Underground (at Westminster) in 1924, were looking for a new and distinctive architecture without fuss or adornment. Prior to the extension of the Piccadilly Line, Pick and Holden toured Europe together to observe the latest innovations in the design of public buildings. They were particularly impressed by what they saw in Scandinavia and the Netherlands.

Arsenal station is the only Underground station named after a football club. Originally Gillespie Road, it was renamed thus in 1932 at the suggestion of the club's management.

Automatic Train Operation The Victoria Line, planned in detail from the late 1950s presented a huge requirement for new staff at a time when it was already hard to recruit staff, and this caused there to be a serious look at automation. London Transport conducted tests from 1962 and having obtained support from the railway inspectorate subject to various safety conditions being met it introduced automatic operation on the Hainault-Woodford service of the Central Line in 1965. This was very successful and a similar system was specified for the Victoria Line, opened in 1968. This became one of the first railways in the world to use fully-featured automatically driven trains, and the system has only recently been superseded.

Stand on the right
No smoking

Because of the expense of conversion to automatic operation it proved more cost efficient to use new technology to introduce one person operation on other lines with a large number of new safety systems coupled with the train radio network (introduced in early 1980s). Automatic operation therefore had to wait until lines were resignalled. Today the Victoria, Central and Jubilee Lines are all automatically driven, and the Northern, Metropolitan and Hammersmith & Circle will follow.

B

Baker Street is the station with the most platforms (ten) in use on London Underground. Its platforms 5 and 6 served the very first section of the Underground on opening in January 1863 and a number of features on these reflect its history.

Bakerloo southwards – a long-awaited extension

Despite aspirations to extend the Bakerloo Line southwards dating back to 1919, the first announcement that construction would go ahead took another 30 years to materialise. Work was due to start in 1950, with trains running in 1953. The line duly appeared on the Underground's 1949 and 1950 map folders as 'under construction'.

The line was to have two stations, an intermediate one at Albany Road (current name, previously named Camberwell Gate) and the terminus at Camberwell Green. Detailed costings made in 1950 showed the extension was unaffordable and the plans were put on hold. Since then London Underground reviewed the plans in 1963 and 1969 and in 2006 the then mayor of London Ken Livingstone promised a tube to Camberwell "within 20 years". In 2015 it became known that the preferred route for an extension of the line had switched away from Camberwell to New Cross via the Old Kent Road. It remains some way in the future.

Bank station is notable in a number of respects. One of its entrances leads down to a ticket hall in the crypt of St Mary Woolnoth church and another is built into the south-west corner of the Bank of England building. The station suffered a direct hit by a high explosive bomb in the 1940 Blitz. It is one of only two tube stations with a moving walkway, the other being Waterloo, and also one of only two with a four-letter name, the other being Oval. The moving walkway, which leads down to the Waterloo & City Line, was the first in Britain and was completed in 1960.

Battersea Power Station station is, along with Nine Elms, part of the newest stretch of the London Underground, being opened on 20 September 2021 with the extension of the Northern Line via a new branch to this major redevelopment from Kennington. It is unique on the Underground in having 'Station' in its name, hence its full name includes the word twice. It is also the longest station name on the London Underground, with 21 letters.

Blow holes. When the London Underground opened in 1863 there was no practical alternative to steam traction. Moreover, it was not only the rail traveller who had to endure the smoky exhaust of the Underground trains. To relieve the atmosphere below ground certain openings that had been provided originally at King's Cross and other stations to improve the lighting there were adapted as smoke vents. Subsequently 'blow holes' were constructed along the route between King's Cross and Edgware Road, with openings covered by gratings in the centre of the roadway above. These were prone to sudden belching of steamy vapour that startled the passing horses. On the southern part of the Circle Line large 'blow holes' were constructed (with the approval of Parliament) in the gardens of the Victoria Embankment between Charing Cross and Waterloo Bridges and near to Temple station. In 1883 public opposition to these 'objectionable blow holes' was such that two bills were proposed in Parliament to force the railway to remove them. The Railway Passengers' Protection Society took an opposing view and in the event nothing was done. In 1898 the scandal of these blowholes was debated afresh, with John Burns, the MP for Battersea declaiming how "our beautiful Embankment can be vandalised by the Underground Railway, with its stinking blow-holes, poisoning the air, and making a hideous eyesore to the Embankment". In reality nothing was or could be done and the ventilators still exist, although no longer belching smoke.

Boston Manor is the only Underground station to have appeared on a British postage stamp, doing so in January 2013 as part of a set of stamps commemorating the 150th anniversary of the system.

Buckingham Palace

Rumours abound that Buckingham Palace has its own private station on the Victoria Line; also that secret tunnels connect the palace to Green Park or Charing Cross stations so that the Royal Family can escape in case of war or insurrection. All of them are unfounded but if you take the public tour of Buckingham Palace today you will see in one of the exhibit sections a genuine London Underground 'roundel' station sign with the name Buckingham Palace. However, this is not evidence of the legendary secret station but a souvenir that was presented to the late Queen after she visited Aldgate station on 24 February 2010.

Busking. Buskers discovered the Tube in the late 1970s, being mentioned in the sixth edition of the book *Alternative London* (1982) but not in previous printings. The book cites London Transport byelaw 22 as the only specific law making busking illegal and adds that if you do get arrested, the worst penalty is usually a £10 fine. On the Underground entertainers were considered a nuisance, like beggars, especially when they also obstructed narrow passageways with their pitch. Responding to public opinion London Underground relented in 2003 after 80 per cent of passengers questioned said they enjoyed live music. A trial licensing musicians to perform on tube stations soon became permanent and today passengers enjoy more than 100,000 hours of live music performed every year by professional, talented buskers. The performers have a unique audience of around 3.5 million Tube passengers every day, many of whom show their appreciation by dropping a few coins in the busker's hat. For some buskers this activity can be lucrative too. The web page *Make Money Busking* states: "Of course a bad busker could make nothing at all but a good ones claim they can make up to £40 an hour. Others talk of making £150 per day so for some it's a full time job."

Busking on the tube can also be the stepping stone to greater things. The scheme has attracted international media interest and some buskers are booked regularly for events and recording sessions; some have even gone on to perform in front of royalty or work with established musicians ranging from Simply Red to principals of the English National Opera. The lure of performing on the Tube has also attracted some big names. The Libertines, Julian Lloyd-Webber, Badly Drawn Boy and Seasick Steve have all played on the Underground's stage.

C

Camden Town station has a now unique Underground roundel logo above the east side entrance, being all red instead of red and blue. This dates from the early 1970s when a design consultant specified that all roundels should be in a single colour. The idea was dropped a few years later. It is also another of the stations with a wartime deep level shelter, one of whose two entrances can be found in Buck Street at the rear of the station (the other is demolished).

Carpets on Underground trains Train services run by the Metropolitan Railway extended some distance out into the countryside with some quite long journeys, Liverpool Street to Aylesbury could easily take an hour and a half. To make journeys more tolerable for those prepared to pay for them the company entered into discussion with the Pullman Car Company to offer Pullman facilities on certain trains. The decision was at least in part the result of competition from the Great Central Railway who ran services over the same tracks. The Pullman company (originally American but with significant British interests) made the first approach and offered to provide and operate two Pullman cars from 1910 for a fixed term, making it worthwhile to build two special cars (in fact constructed as part of a wider batch of ten). The Pullman company was remunerated by sales of food and drink, and by a Pullman supplement that was charged for using the cars, 6d for journeys south of Rickmansworth and a shilling for anyone travelling to or from points further north. The supplement went to Pullmans. The Metropolitan maintained the cars and the cooking facilities and did not charge for haulage.

The cars were deep-pile carpeted and well up to the usual Pullman standard and like other first class cars were named; the names received were Mayflower and Galatea. They were at first painted Pullman's normal umber and cream but this did not wear well and were soon painted red.

The cars normally operated between London and either Chesham or Aylesbury (in early days Quainton Road), but occasionally ventured further north for operational convenience, though not in service. The cars always operated in separate trains. In 1918 the main trains were 8:1 am Quainton Road to Aldgate and 4:56 pm Liverpool Street to Chesham (Mayflower) and 9:26am Great Missenden to Liverpool Street, 5:29pm Liverpool Street to Aylesbury (Galatea). This car also operated a late train 11:15pm Baker Street to Aylesbury. Depending on time of day breakfast, tea or a light supper was available as well as a range of drinks.

Incompatible with London Transport's 1930s aspirations for modernisation of the Metropolitan, the agreement was allowed to lapse when the Second World War broke out and the cars were recovered by Pullmans and the bodies disposed of (becoming a timber merchant's office at Hinchley Wood).

The Pullman cars were not the only cars to sport carpets though, as all the Metropolitan Railway's first class compartments had them, at least until first class was abolished during the Second World War. Carpets do not take kindly to the Underground environment and traditionally wooden floors have been used as they are easy to sweep and wash. With wood (even fireproof wood) increasingly frowned upon, and expensive, new floor surfaces have been tested over the years and a carpet was tried in a Piccadilly Line car in 1974 but failed to give satisfaction. Since the 1980s composite flooring has been provided and seems to meet modern requirements for wear, slip, cleanability and fire prevention.

Chalk Farm station. For fans of the classic Leslie Green surface buildings of 1906/7, the station has the longest frontage of any.

Chancery Lane station was the site of Kingsway telephone exchange until the 1980s, constructed within a deep level air-raid shelter built below it during the Second World War.

Clapham Common and neighbouring **Clapham North** stations are the only ones on the Underground remaining with original, and fairly narrow, island platforms (i.e. a single platform at each serving trains in both directions) at tube tunnel level. There were five of these when the Northern Line (as it is today) was built, the other three being at Angel, Euston and Stockwell. Modern island platforms, such as those at Canada Water and Canary Wharf, are much wider.

Closed circuit TV on the Underground
There are currently (2013) more than 12,000 CCTV cameras on the Tube network, a figure that will rise to more than 14,000 over the next few years as part of the ongoing station modernisation programme. This will see the upgrading and expansion of CCTV facilities from analogue to digital and the recording of high quality images to hard drive rather than magnetic tape.

These cameras, which can be operated centrally as well as locally, are a vital means of maintaining London's transport system as a safe and low-crime environment and ensuring that crime rates continue to fall.

The first CCTV installation on the Underground was in 1961, when five black and white cameras were installed to monitor passenger movement in the main circulating areas at Holborn station. Widespread implementation took place during the 1990s, when London Underground embarked on a programme of blanket CCTV coverage across its then 250-station network. A subsequent innovation was the 'track to train CCTV system' that enables train operators to view pictures of the platform approaching each station and once in the station, monitor the doors and passenger safety from the cab.

Covent Garden station has often in the past been threatened with closure owing to its proximity to Leicester Square station and below average usage. Today it is a very busy station serving the retail outlets that have sprung up in modern times around the old Covent Garden fruit, vegetable and flower market. The distance between it and its Leicester Square neighbour is not the shortest on the Underground (0.161 miles, 259.3 metres) but is the second shortest after the distance between Charing Cross and Embankment on the Northern Line (0.111 miles, 180 metres).

Creature comforts in wartime. At the height the second world war bombing raids some 80 tube stations played host to thousands of families in London, grateful for the protection they afforded, even though a direct hit could—and did on two occasions —penetrate down to tube platforms. An eye-witness account of the time described: "By 4pm all the platforms and passage space of the underground station are staked out, chiefly with blankets folded in long strips laid against the wall—for the trains are still running and the platforms in use. A woman or child guards places for about six people. When the evening comes, the rest of the family crowd in." A warden added, "The atmosphere is generally a friendly one. Disputes are determined by the station staff, police, or wardens, with the surrounding shelterers as an unofficial jury of comment. By eleven most of the shelterers are asleep. Maintenance gangs still carry on their work on track and cables and clear the litter which a few careless hands still throw on the track." There were a few problems when passengers had to clamber over shelterers but the number of late evening passengers was much reduced because of the black-out and the fact that many businesses had relocated to outside the centre of London.

A number of creature comforts were provided to make the life of shelterers more amenable. Snacks and hot drinks, delivered by special tube trains, were served nightly, and at some stations there were even libraries, recorded music played on gramophones provided by American charities and live entertainment. The 'scheme for refreshment service' was introduced in October 1940 and by December catering facilities were fully operational at 80 stations and using specially converted trains to deliver the refreshments, a service that continued until May 1945. Toilets linked to sewage apparatus were also installed.

LONDON TRANSPORT in conjunction with The LOCAL AUTHORITY

Admit one Person for Shelter
(if available) at
EARLS COURT (Picc) Station

Persons permitted to use this Station as, or as a means of access to, an Air Raid Shelter do so at their own risk in all respects.

FOR FURTHER CONDITIONS SEE BACK

52694

Cut and cover or bored — two ways of building tunnels. Nearly all of the below-surface lines of the London Underground were dug either by *bored tunnelling* or *cut and cover* methods. Cut and cover was used first, so we'll begin with this technique.

Cut and cover was the only way of constructing shallow tunnels, such as those found on the Circle Line, in Victorian times. Construction begins by excavating a trench and then roofing over it. The covering must be strong enough to carry the load of what is to be built above the tunnel, which may be a roadway or some kind of building. Nowadays large cut-and-cover boxes are often used instead of bored tunnelling for Underground stations, such as Canary Wharf (Jubilee Line) and the new Northern Ticket Hall at King's Cross. The tunnel boring machine illustrated above was used on the Northern Line extension to Battersea Power Station.

Bored tunnelling using a tunnelling shield (*shown opposite*) is the method for the deep-level or tube lines. The shield is a protective structure used for excavating tunnels through ground that may be unstable. As the shield is pushed forward it cuts a circular opening that is then lined with a support structure of concrete, cast iron or steel. The early deep tunnels of the Underground were dug manually by workers protected by the shield, which itself was moved forward by powerful jacks. Nowadays a tunnel boring machine is used, consisting of a shield with a rotating cutting wheel and a system for removing the excavated soil mechanically. Hydraulic jacks are used to push the machine forward.

D

Deepest and highest. The maximum depth below ground level is on the Northern Line at Holly Bush Hill, Hampstead: 221 feet (68.8 metres). Nearby Hampstead station is the deepest station on the network at 192 feet (58.5 metres) below street level. To reach the platforms you use the deepest lifts on the system, descending 181 feet (55.2 metres). The overall lowest point on the system is at Westminster on the Jubilee Line, where the tracks are 105 feet (32 metres) below sea level. The highest point reached by London Underground trains is near Amersham on the Metropolitan Line at about 500 feet (150 metres) above sea level. The greatest elevation from ground level is reached on the Dollis Brook viaduct on the Mill Hill East branch of the Northern Line, 60 feet (18 metres) above Dollis Road below.

Deep Shelters Locations were sought in 1940 by the Ministry of Home Security for deep shelters to protect civilians in London. By building these at locations below existing tube stations, it was felt that non-stopping trains could by-pass them by means of the tube profile shelters upon connection to the existing line after the war. The ten shelters, using tube tunnel components and accommodating 9,600 persons in bunks, were to be located at Belsize Park, Camden Town *(below)*, Chancery Lane, Goodge Street, St Paul's, Clapham Common, Clapham North, Clapham South, Oval and Stockwell. All except St Paul's and Oval were completed. At Oval construction was halted because water ingress was so persistent that it would have made further construction prohibitively expensive. At St Paul's the cathedral authorities objected that the tunnelling might damage the foundations of the cathedral.

Occupation by civilians did not begin until mid-1944 and the first use of these shelters was in 1943, for billeting troops on leave. Some of the shelters were reserved for government purposes entirely. Camden Town was used as a hostel for troops from 1943 to 1947. Chancery Lane was

equipped as working and sleeping accommodation for key government staff and also used as military hostel and later by security services (subsequently it was opened as Kingsway telephone exchange in 1954, being used for storage only from 1990 onwards). Clapham Common was used during the war as a hostel for American troops. Clapham South was used as weekend troop accommodation from 1943 during the war and afterwards, as leave hostel from June 1945, as armed forces troop billets in 1946; as a hostel for Jamaican immigrants in 1948; as the Festival Hotel for provincial visitors to London in 1951, as a troop billet for the funeral of King George VI in 1952 and finally as accommodation for Coronation visitors in 1953. Goodge Street was used by U.S and British forces from 1943 to 1945 and as an armed forces hostel from 1947 until the disastrous fire of 1956. Stockwell was used by British and U.S. troops as a hostel during the war, as a leave hostel from 1945 and then for museum and record storage from 1947 until May 1951.

Ironically, the tunnels were never used as bypass tube lines (the acute economic austerity that followed the end of hostilities meant there was no money to finance building of new railways). The tunnels built as deep shelters are owned by TfL and have various uses today, typically for document or computer data storage.

Did you forget something? Every day more than 1,000 TfL passengers leave things behind – and around 300 get something back. The rest remains in the Lost Property Office for three months, after which the items are given to charity or sent for auction. Most commonly lost items are mobile phones; the strangest including a park bench, samurai swords, a lawnmower, worn underwear, false teeth, a grandfather clock, a stuffed fox, breast implants and prosthetic limbs. The office, which also takes in items found on buses, is located in Baker Street, almost opposite the fictional base of Sherlock Holmes, which explains why the computer system that logs lost items is nicknamed 'Sherlock'.

Disused stations. The number of 'ghost' stations on the London Underground extends to several score, the exact number depending on how creatively you determine the eligibility for inclusion. Categories include stations that were planned (in some cases partially or fully constructed) but not opened; were closed because of declining passenger numbers; were made redundant after a replacement was constructed nearby; are no longer served by Underground trains but remain open to other companies' trains; or are used by staff trains only and are not open to the public.

A couple of these closed stations still see use for filming purposes, these being Aldwych and Charing Cross (Jubilee Line). In many cases the platforms are removed after stations are closed, with the surface buildings either demolished for redevelopment or sold to new owners for alternative roles as retail premises, restaurants or even residential use. Sometimes street level station buildings are made redundant when a new entrance is constructed in subways below the roadway. Buildings that remain recognisable include Aldwych, Brompton Road, Hyde Park Corner, Marlborough Road *(below)*, South Kentish Town and York Road. *For more details see the book London's Disused Underground Stations 978-185414-467-6*

Drinking on the Underground. These days you will not find a licensed bar inside a London Underground station, nor can you drink alcohol on trains or Underground premises, but this was not always the case. In fact Sloane Square was the last place to have a licensed bar at platform level (the Hole in the Wall, closed in 1985). It was by no means the only place you could enjoy a pint on the Underground either. According to the book Underground London, there were more than 30 licensed buffets on the Underground at the time of the First World War. Some of these on the Circle Line, at Baker Street, Mansion House and Liverpool Street, lasted until the 1960s and 1970s. The closest you can come to drinking at an Underground station now is The Metropolitan Bar, which is located at first floor level above Baker Street station and open seven days a week from 8am to 11pm.

Between 1910 and 1939 another way of buying a drink on the Underground was to travel in the comfort of a Pullman Car. A couple of Pullmans were included in certain Metropolitan Line trains that ran between London via Amersham to Aylesbury. As well as alcoholic drinks, patrons could enjoy tea and coffee, with lunch and snacks served on the daytime services and a light supper on the late train.

E

East Finchley's archer statue, on the north east side of the station, was intended to be the first of a number of statues at stations on the Northern Line, including Dick Whittington for Highgate and a Roman centurion at Elstree South (both unbuilt).The unfulfilled plans for Highgate station involved a much more substantial station building than the unambitious structures that were eventually built.

Elephant & Castle station is where the first baby to be born on a London tube line came into the world. Marie Cordery was born there in 1924. A false story put about at the time, and often quoted since, claims that she was called Thelma Ursula Beatrice Eleanor after the Tube. The Northern Line entrance to the station is about 250 metres from the Bakerloo Line entrance and separated by one of the largest roundabouts in London, on which is a structure containing an electrical substation for the Northern Line and a memorial to electricity pioneer Michael Faraday.

Elizabeth Line is London's latest tube railway construction, linking the main lines at Paddington and Liverpool Street and adding a new route to Abbey Wood via Canary Wharf. The tunnels were built with the use of eight 7-metre diameter tunnel boring machines with kitchen and toilets inside so that operators could spend the whole working day in them. Each of the shields was given a female name. One was called Phyllis after Phyllis Pearsall, the originator of the A-Z street guides. Victoria and Elizabeth are two of the other names, celebrating the long serving female British monarchs. Mary and Sophia were the names of the wives of railway engineer Isambard Kingdom Brunel and the builder of the first tunnel under the Thames, Marc Brunel. Ada is named after Ada Lovelace, the proto-computer programmer. The line, originally known as Crossrail, has been the largest engineering project in Europe and has 37 stations, eight of these being entirely new sub-surface stations. Within inner London, new Elizabeth Line stations are at Paddington, Bond Street, Tottenham Court Road, Farringdon, Liverpool Street, Whitechapel and Canary Wharf, built on a scale not seen since the Jubilee Line Extension opened in 1999. Some 28 existing Network Rail stations in outer London and suburbs are being upgraded for the new service.

Each of the Elizabeth Line's new trains is able to accommodate up to 1,500 passengers in a length of 200 metres, carrying an estimated 200 million passengers per year. The line is sometimes thought to be part of the Underground but it is a separate railway, like London Overground.

ELIZABETH LINE

Escalators. The escalators on the London Underground are something we take for granted — all 400-plus of them. Escalators, originally known as moving stairs, have been a part of the London Underground for more than a hundred years. Originally tube stations were equipped only with lifts but these have many disadvantages, including an irritating wait for the lift to arrive, the need (in those days) for an attendant to operate each lift and the inability to handle large numbers of passengers rapidly. All these disadvantages were eliminated by the escalator.

The mechanical design of the escalator has changed little over the years; a chain of individual and linked steps are driven by motors to move up or down on tracks in a way that the treads of the steps always remain horizontal. The advantages of this system are manifold. Large numbers of people can be moved in a short time and a flight of escalators occupies little more space than that taken by an equivalent fixed staircase, apart from a motor chamber underneath.

The first escalator on the London Underground was brought into service at Earl's Court station in 1911, where a pair of escalators was brought into use linking the Piccadilly and District Line platforms. Given the novelty of a moving staircase it is not surprising that some passengers did not feel inclined to try this new means of transportation. There is a story that to counter their misgivings and demonstrate the complete safety of the escalator a one-legged man by the name of 'Bumper Harris' was directed to travel up and down the escalator. Some uncertainty surrounds this but his great-great grandson Aaron Harris explains that he worked on the Underground and: "While working some of his friends played a rather unfortunate joke on him and his leg was crushed between two carriages carrying rubble and he lost his leg. He was then employed to ride the escalator at Earl's Court".

The total number of escalators on the Underground is 426. The longest escalators on the Underground, as mentioned earlier, are at Angel. The shortest are at Stratford, with a vertical rise of 4.1 metres.

Emergency escape. Nobody wishes to become stuck on a tube train that has broken down but if you are wondering about the procedure for evacuating trains, it's all very practical and straightforward.

The first thing the train operator must do after informing passengers by the public address system is to report the situation and summon assistance. This is done by radio communication between the driver and the line controller. The next thing is for the 630-volt traction current to be switched off. Turning off the current automatically turns on the tunnel lights and sets all signals to danger in the vicinity of the breakdown.

When trains break down it may not be necessary for passengers to leave the train. It may be possible to arrange for the stranded train to be pushed to the next station by another train.

F

Fairlop, under late 1930s plans, would have been one of two Central Line stations serving a major London Airport that was planned for Fairlop Plain, located between Fairlop and Hainault. The station would probably have been resited to better suit the layout of the planned airport.

Faraway Places. Which point in central London is furthest from a tube station? This was a question asked by *The Guardian* newspaper in 2012. Answers provided by readers were the junction of King's Road and Old Church Street in Chelsea, the Albert Memorial in the south of Kensington Gardens, or else the duck pond in Battersea Park.

The station furthest south is Morden (Northern Line) and the station furthest east is Upminster on the District Line (until 1939 you could travel all the way to Southend on Sea on certain District Line trains). Chesham on the Metropolitan Line is both the northernmost and westernmost station on the current network.

Fantastic factory. During the Second World War factories were built underground to safeguard production for strategically vital industries, such as for aircraft manufacture. One of the most unusual facilities, described after the war as a 'fantastic factory', was constructed in tunnels built (but not yet completed) for an extension of the Underground's Central Line from Liverpool Street to Epping. After the war it was nominated as the most successful underground factory in the country.

In twin tunnels just under two and a half miles long, the production facilities occupied 300,000 sq ft of floor space and employed a total of 2,000 workers (mainly female) in shifts 24 hours around the clock. Miniature trains hauled by battery locomotives ran along an 18in gauge railway in each bore to transport materials. Workers entered the underground factory at the unfinished Gants Hill, Redbridge and Wanstead station sites, using the stairs provided at Redbridge and escalators at the other two. Products carried out underground included wiring looms for Halifax and Lancaster bombers, a quarter of a million aircraft pumps, wireless equipment, 22,000 cartridge starters for fighters, gear levers for armoured vehicles, shell fuses and field telephones.

Observers describing this strange workplace commented on the unending vista of equally spaced lights in the circular tunnel. Down one side stood the long single row of machines tended by young ladies in their white overalls, while on the other ran the 18-inch track carrying 'a very serviceable train on its endless journey of fetch and carry'. Discussion of the factory and its working was forbidden during the war and during this period entry was by production of a pass only. Strict secrecy was observed and even now some of the Plessey pensioners are reluctant to speak about their experience. No public announcement of what went on was made until March 1946 and the only clue that observant bystanders would have seen at the time was the windowless factory buildings and the sheds full of bicycles.

Fastest trains on the Underground are on the Jubilee Line. On parts of the extension to Stratford the maximum running speed is 60mph. Elsewhere on the system maxima of 40–50mph are more typical.

Finchley Central was used in the 1930s by Harry Beck and features a commemorative plaque on the southbound platform together with a facsimile of Beck's original Underground diagram of 1933.

Finsbury Park station has its own on-site police station, as do Wembley Park and Stockwell.

First class travel. When the London Underground opened in 1863 it was only natural that it should offer the three options of first, second and third class travel, exactly as many of the above-ground railways did. When the Metropolitan District Railway (today's District Line) opened five years later it followed suit. Second class was withdrawn on the District Line in 1903 and in 1905 on the Metropolitan, whereas first class was not entirely withdrawn until 1941.

Fleet Line — sunk without trace. When planned in the early 1970s, the intention was that this new line should take over the Stanmore branch of the Bakerloo Line as far as Baker Street, then head south in new tunnels to Bond Street, Green Park and Charing Cross, then east via Aldwych, Ludgate Circus, Cannon Street and Fenchurch Street before striking off south towards New Cross and Lewisham. Financial authority was available to construct the line as far as Charing Cross and construction began in 1971, with completion under its new Jubilee Line name in 1979. It had been renamed in 1977 to commemorate HM the Queen's silver jubilee.

Floodgates Historically, floodgates (movable gates used for controlling water flow) have played an important role in protecting the deep tube lines of London Underground from inundation. At the beginning of the 1939-45 war a total of 21 floodgates were installed to isolate parts of the tunnel network to prevent flooding if nearby rivers or sewers were breached. Since the completion of the Thames flood barrier at Woolwich in the 1980s the risk to the Underground is considered much reduced and regular testing of the floodgates ceased. Some of the gates are now locked against operation or welded open, with the special floodgate telephones and detection circuits removed.

- The 1939 floodgates were installed at South Kensington, Embankment, Charing Cross, Waterloo, London Road, London Bridge, Wapping, Bethnal Green and Bank.
- The 1950s floodgates were installed at Russell Square, Tottenham Court Road, Green Park, Kennington, Moorgate and Liverpool Street.
- The 1960s floodgates were installed at Green Park on the Victoria Line.
- In the 1990s floodgates were installed at Canning Town on the Jubilee Line.

Two floodgates remain in use on the tube, as well as low-level flood barriers that can be used at station entrances. For security reasons no more details are available.

Freight on the Underground. Goods trains ran on the Underground until the 1960s. Steam trains delivered meat to Smithfield Meat Market until July 1962, running mostly at night to avoid delaying passenger trains. Steam-hauled trains also delivered coal to many goods yards at Underground stations including East Finchley, Finchley Central, Woodside Park, Totteridge and High Barnet until October 1962. The yards were then converted into car parks for underground train passengers. The luxury apartments at Chiltern Court (Baker Street) also had their own coal trains, the last of which ran in August 1961.

Fossils on the Underground. The blue clay beneath London is not particularly rich in fossils, but they do sometimes appear during tunnelling work. The construction of the Northern line tunnel from Archway to East Finchley in 1939 uncovered a fossilised crab with very well-preserved eyes, claws, and legs. Six fossilised nautiloids some fifty million years old were found during construction of the Victoria line near Victoria station. They are now residents of the Natural History Museum.

Four million was the total number of passengers carried each working day on the Underground at its peak in the first two decades of the 21st Century. Post-Covid, this had dropped to an average of two million per day.

Furthest-flung tube tunnels and escalators. The most westerly London Underground tunnels lie 29 miles west of London in deepest Surrey, underneath the club house of Wentworth golf course (near Virginia Water). Twin cast-iron Tube tunnels 100 yards long were installed there during the Second World War, using surplus components marked LPTB (London Passenger Transport Board). The tunnels were used as a protected signals centre by the 21st Army Group in the lead up to D-Day.

The location is just south of Wentworth House (now the club house for the golf course). The whole construction is protected on the surface by a massive bombproof 'burster' slab with a brick ventilation cowl protruding. The slab itself is now used as a car park.

A couple of escalators made an even longer journey in 1941, when they were commandeered for use at a giant underground factory and ammunition depot at Corsham, near Bath. A letter dated 24 June 1941 in the National Archive records that the London Passenger Transport Board would loan the Ministry of Aircraft Production two escalators for installation in an underground factory in the west of England. One of these had been destined for the top flight of escalators at Highgate station (deferred because of war) and the letter proposed that one of the upper flight from St

Paul's be removed to provide the second. In the event Holborn No.4 and No.6 from St Paul's were used and an escalator at the east end of Spring Quarry, Corsham still exists (in very poor condition now) bearing a large brass plate on its gearbox saying 'Holborn No. 4'.

G

Garden produce. A number of stations have flower gardens or vegetable allotments tended by the staff in their spare time and there is also an annual *Underground In Bloom* competition entered by up to a quarter of the stations and depots enter every year. The annual competition, which dates back to the early 1920s at least, aims to recognise employees who spend much of their free time creating a pleasant and colourful environment for their colleagues to enjoy. Their work also helps to improve the local environment, encourages flora and fauna and makes travelling more pleasant for passengers.

Categories traditionally include Hanging Baskets, Tubs and Best Overall Garden. In 2010 a new Fruit and Vegetable category was introduced in support of the Mayor's Capital Growth programme, which encourages communities and organisations to grow their own food, whilst the following year the judges awarded additional points for 'greener' gardens. A separate award recognises special achievement, such as at Hampstead where despite challenging conditions, the staff managed to grow over 20 varieties of fruit and vegetables (including jalapeno peppers and strawberries) in a small area at the back of the building.

Gladstone's coffin. The coffin of Victorian statesman William Gladstone was carried by train on the District Line between Kensington Olympia and Westminster in 1898, but not in an Underground train as is often claimed. It was in a London & North Western train hauled by a London Brighton

& South Coast railway locomotive named Gladstone. It took the coffin along the District on the final part of the train's journey to Westminster Hall for his body to lie in state prior to his state funeral at Westminster Abbey. The coffin was moved from Westminster station to the Hall via a direct subway that exists between the two. It is often claimed, incorrectly, that the coffin of Dr Barnardo was also carried on an Underground train, but it was in fact carried on a Great Eastern Railway line, part of which was later taken over by London Transport.

Gloucester Road is a good example of the origins of the Underground in separate private companies rather than the unified system that exists today. The original Piccadilly Line station building abuts the earlier Metropolitan District Railway station and to interchange between the District/ Circle Lines and the Piccadilly, passengers need to walk up two flights of stairs to ground level to reach lifts that take them down to the Piccadilly platforms. A similar juxtaposition of street level buildings can be found at neighbouring South Kensington station, though interchange between the lines is easier here.

Going green. Despite the Underground name, half of the network in fact runs above ground. What's more, it provides ten per cent of the city's wildlife habitat for over 1,000 animal and plant species. The 4,000 hectares of land that surround the Tube's rail tracks act as a safe haven for a huge variety of the Capital's wildlife, including bats, badgers, reptiles, stag beetles and water voles. Passengers travelling on the Jubilee Line between Wembley Park and Kingsbury may have noticed some unusual looking boxes springing up on the trackside near Fryent Country Park. These boxes, which provide homes for solitary bees, are just one example of a wide variety of biodiversity protection projects that are being carried out on the Underground.

The Underground's first 'green' initiative was in 1909, when it was reported: "London's underground railway stations, once noted for their dirt and gloom, are to be transformed by flowers and baskets of ferns and evergreens. Keeping the stations clean became possible only when the system was electrified, and the floral decorations, although only as an experiment to begin with, are expected to complete the transformation."

Graffiti. *"Graffiti on the Tube is not acceptable. It is intimidating and threatening to passengers – in short, it is psychological mugging. In the last two years, we have stepped up the fight against graffiti on the Tube, which costs £20 million each year to clear up. We are working closely with the British Transport Police, Tube Lines and Metronet to cut this crime."*

So said London Underground's managing director in 2005, when the company sued a graffiti vandal successfully for £3,000, the first time it had used civil action to recover the costs of graffiti crimes. These days multiple methods are used to deter graffiti and other acts of criminal damage on the Tube network. British Transport Police collaborates too in order to ensure incidents are investigated thoroughly and Transport for London has invested to increase the numbers of police patrolling the Tube network to its highest ever level of more than 700 officers. At the same time it has also increased the number of CCTV cameras to more than 12,000. The security perimeters around its land and depots are upgraded regularly with intruder detection systems to keep premises secure. London Underground devotes significant and growing resources to visible policing across the transport system, to ensure that it continues to deliver an environment where passengers feel comfortable and safe.

Grand designs. The Underground attracts some unusual schemes from visionaries, three of which deserve mentioning here. The Hanging Gardens of Bayswater were proposed in 2010 to make proper use of the empty space above the Circle Line cutting behind Leinster Gardens (see *Nothing but a Façade* later in this book). Architects proposed a public open space above the railway where local people could grow vegetables in glasshouses and on allotments and recycle waste food, irrigated by a large rainwater catcher. The scheme received a Commended award in the Forgotten Spaces competition of the Royal Institution of British Architects but was not built.

A scheme that has become reality is the Green Wall at Edgware Road tube station for trapping harmful pollution from particulates in road traffic exhausts. Around 180 square metres of vegetation cover the wall of the Bakerloo Line station, adjacent to Marylebone Road. Scientists state that planting living 'green walls' of grass tufts, ivy and other climbing plants could provide a faster and cheaper way of cleaning up the air in cities than large-scale initiatives such as congestion charging. Transport for London installed the green walls as part of a package of short-term measures introduced where particulate levels are at their highest.

Green Park station is near Buckingham Palace and where Queen Elizabeth II officially opened the central section of the Victoria Line on 7 March 1969. Embarrassingly, the automatic ticket machine at Green Park rejected her money when she attempted to buy a ticket as part of her tour of the new technology. After a short ceremony on the platform, the Queen entered the driving cab of a waiting train and pushed the button to start it for a short journey to Victoria.

Greenford has the only wooden escalator still installed at an Underground station. This is because it is above ground and so not regarded as a fire-safety issue. The station is also unusual in having a main line track (for a shuttle service running from there to Paddington via Ealing Broadway) between the two Central Line platforms.

H

Hampstead station platforms and lift shafts are the deepest below ground level on the system. The platforms are 192ft below ground and anyone using the emergency stairs will find that they have a tube record high of 320 steps.

Harrow and Ruislip. These two towns in north-west London share the distinction of being the only ones on the Underground to each have five stations: Harrow & Wealdstone, Harrow-on-the-Hill, North Harrow, South Harrow, West Harrow, and Ruislip, Ruislip Gardens, Ruislip Manor, South Ruislip, West Ruislip.

Harrow & Wealdstone is the only station served by the Underground to have been the scene of a major main line train crash. On 8 October 1952 two expresses and a local train were involved in a crash here, causing 112 fatalities, on lines that parallel the Bakerloo Line. This was the worst peacetime disaster on Britain's railways.

Heathrow Airport Terminal 5 Underground station is owned and operated by Heathrow Airport. It is one of six stations served by Underground trains but not owned by the Underground, the others being Barking, Ealing Broadway, Richmond, Willesden Junction and Wimbledon.

Heritage. London Underground has its own full time Heritage Manager who looks after stations 'listed' by English Heritage or local authorities as well as smaller items of design interest on the system such as old signs, clocks and lamps. Many of these smaller items are replicas, newly made to suit the architecture of particular stations.

Hidden secrets. Reconstruction or change of purpose mean that several stations have areas that occasionally come to light but are not open to the public (for safety and insurance reasons visits cannot be permitted). For instance, although the lifts at Notting Hill Gate station were removed and replaced by escalators in 1959, a passageway leading to the lifts survives. A dozen or more colourful posters survive untouched by the fingers of time, creating a miniature museum of advertising of the late fifties.

At Liverpool Street (Circle Line) station a doorway is occasionally left open on the footbridge, providing glimpses of daylight at the far end of a long passageway leading to an old exit from the station.

The original King's Cross (Circle Line) station was situated below King's Cross Bridge; trains still pass its disused platforms. An underground passageway still runs below the streets from here all the way to the concourse of King's Cross stations (its continuation to St Pancras station was destroyed when the new Western Ticket Hall was constructed). Many other tube stations have passages that are now disused.

At South Kensington there is a tube station that was half-built but never opened. Intended for a relief tube line bypassing the District Line between Earl's Court and Mansion House, with just one intermediate station at Charing Cross, the construction was a victim of changed plans and only one platform was completed before work ceased. During the First World War the location was used for storing treasures from the Victoria & Albert Museum as well as china from Buckingham Palace. Afterwards it was used for staff training, fitted out with track and signals. Later it was used in World War Two as an emergency headquarters for the Underground's engineering services.

Hounslow East is at the start of a section of the tube with the highest number of consecutive stations (six) with the same initial letter.

I

Initial letters of the alphabet with no Underground stations are J, X, Y and Z. Until 1932 there was a Piccadilly Line station at York Road, near King's Cross station. There are no place names in London beginning with the letters J, X or Z. However, every letter of the alphabet appears in the name of an Underground station somewhere.

Iron Oxide comprises two-thirds of the dust in London tube tunnels, according to the New Scientist. It is mainly produced by abrasion between train wheels and the track.

J

Johnston - Just our type. The elegant and still modern-looking typeface used throughout the London Underground on signs, posters and other publicity was originally designed during the First World War. Edward Johnston, whose students included Eric Gill, was commissioned by the Underground company in 1915 to design a distinctive typeface for its use. Modified in 1980 and renamed New Johnston, this was replaced by a more sympathetic reworking of the original Johnston in 2016. New Johnston remains widespread on station signs and an example is shown below.

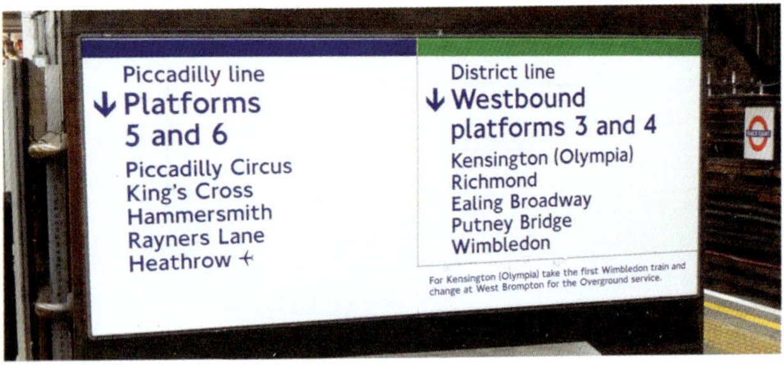

Jubilee Line. The extension to Canary Wharf and Stratford arose from an original proposal for a privately funded express tube from Waterloo to Canary Wharf. The developers of Canary Wharf in the event went into liquidation and paid a very small proportion of the cost.

K

Kennington station is the only remaining example of the architecture of the world's first deep tube line, the City & South London Railway. The station building was designed by T. Phillips Figgis, the company's architect, and like all the other stations built for the new line it is surmounted by a large lead-sheathed dome.

King's Cross St Pancras has the largest number of Underground lines passing through it (five) and is the system's second busiest station (after Waterloo).

Knightsbridge is notable in having six consecutive consonants in it, the only Underground station to do so.

L

Ladies Only. Compartments labelled Ladies Only were a feature of the Metropolitan Line until sometime in the 1950s. They were originally introduced by the Metropolitan Railway back in 1874, but stopped in 1875 owing to lack of use. They were then reintroduced in 1931 and some Metropolitan practices, including this one, continued into London Transport days. The last compartment carriages on the Metropolitan Line were withdrawn in 1962.

Leicester Square station once had the offices of Wisden's cricketing almanac above it and red terracotta tiling still shows their name above a doorway in the south side of the building.

Level crossings on the Underground. Level crossings on the busy above-ground sections of the Underground would not make a happy combination, which is why none exist across public roads. In fact the only level crossing on an electrified tube line was at North Weald station; the road was not a public highway and was for the use of a nearby landowner's farm. The crossing was closed in 1968 but has recently been reinstated cosmetically by the preservationists who today operate the now non-electrified Epping to Ongar line. Several more level crossings existed on what was to become the eastern extension of the Central Line but they were replaced by road flyovers or underpasses and eliminated entirely before the route was electrified by London Underground. On the rural reaches of the steam-worked Metropolitan Line there were many level crossings.

Leytonstone station has a series of wall mosaics commemorating the work of film director Alfred Hitchcock, who was born locally in 1899. These were paid for by the London Borough of Waltham Forest.

Lifts. The escalator was not commercialised until 1900, making lifts the only alternative to stairs at the original tube stations (in which the platforms are typically 60 feet below street level). Even today lifts survive at a number of deep stations where installing escalators would be problematic. Covent Garden, Edgware Road (Bakerloo Line), Goodge Street and Russell Square are examples of stations that still rely on lifts for this reason.

Nowadays lifts operate automatically, without the need for attendants although station staff can be summoned should problems arise. To simplify escape in the case of emergencies lifts are installed in pairs sharing a single shaft; each car has an unmarked door facing the centre of the shaft. If one lift becomes stalled, the other lift can be lowered to the same level and the doors opened, to enable passengers to transfer to the other car. The total number of lifts of the Underground is 164. The deepest lifts shaft is at Hampstead (55.2 metres) and the shallowest at King's Cross (2.3 metres), the latter a modern one installed for use by the disabled.

Literary connections. It's little wonder that the Underground has found its way into numerous short stories and novels as well as children's story books not to mention countless television programmes and feature films. One of the earliest writers to include the novelty of the Underground was Sir Arthur Conan Doyle, several of whose Sherlock Holmes stories involved travel by this means, even though Holmes himself preferred the hansom cab. His client Alexander Holder, in *The Adventure of the Beryl Coronet* (published 1892), states, "I came to Baker Street by the Underground." In the *Red-Headed League* (1891) Watson tells Holmes, "We travelled by the Underground as far as Aldersgate." Meanwhile in *The Adventure of the Bruce-Partington Plans* the dead body of Cadogan West is discovered by a platelayer just outside Aldgate station, and the subsequent detail shows that Conan Doyle knew plenty about the operation of the Metropolitan Railway.

One of Conan Doyle's contemporaries was the Baroness Orczy, a Hungarian-born British novelist best known for her series of novels featuring *The Scarlet Pimpernel*. She also wrote a dozen detective novels, of which her 1901 story *The Mysterious Death on the Underground Railway* features a lady passenger who is poisoned in a first class compartment, her dead body being discovered at Aldgate station.

Turning to tales written for children, one of the most imaginative was by Algernon Blackwood, describing a breathtakingly surreal tube trip not by train but by elephant in his book titled *By Underground*.

Comprehensive literary listings can be found at Wikipedia on the Internet in the articles 'London Underground in popular culture' and 'List of London Underground-related fiction'.

Liverpool Street Central Line station was, in 1911, the first Underground station to be built with escalators incorporated in the design (the existing station at Earl's Court had had them installed shortly before).

Longest lived names on the Underground are Baker Street and Edgware Road, both stations on the original section of the Underground opened in January 1863. The other stations on the original line have been subject to renaming.

Longest name on the map. As already stated, Battersea Power Station is the longest Underground station name but it is not the longest name on the Underground map. This honour goes to Caledonian Road & Barnsbury on London Overground with 24 characters.

Longest possible journey without changing train. This would be from Epping to West Ruislip on the Central Line (34.1 miles or 54.9km). Take a book to read (such as this one)!

M

Mail Rail — a slumbering giant

As long ago as 1900 the success of London's tube railways did not go unnoticed by the Post Office, whose vans were hindered by the same traffic congestion that made buses and trams so slow. Plans were drawn up for a dedicated tube railway for carrying the mails using electric trains below the streets of London. Unlike existing tube railways, the scheme was to use much smaller tunnels, narrower gauge tracks using driverless trains. In 1911 it was decided to go ahead and to construct a double track tube railway connecting two main line railway stations and several sorting offices along a six-mile east-west axis from Whitechapel to Paddington. Construction was not rapid and tunnel boring did not begin until 1915 and material and labour shortages meant the railway did not become operational until 1928.

The line's planners were vindicated and the railway was a resounding success. In its busiest era the line was carrying an average of four million letters every day between the nine stations along the route, operating 19 hours a day for 286 days a year. In later years new sorting offices were opened away from the route of Mail Rail, as it became known, reducing its value to the Post Office. Other contributory factors were the fact that letter mails no longer came into London by train and the restructuring of London's postal service meant that many of the sorting offices served by Mail Rail had been replaced by vast new mail centres located in the suburbs. The equipment was also well past its prime.

These factors led to the system's closure, which took place on 30 May 2003. Since then the line has been mothballed, with no firm proposals published for its future. In 2011 curators from the British Postal Museum & Archive retrieved examples of rolling stock from Mail Rail for conservation.

Making an exhibition. For 50 years Charing Cross station (now named Embankment) was the setting for exhibitions intended to interest passengers. Certainly the strangest was the display in 1929 of stuffed animals that had met an untimely end on the tracks of the Underground. Otters, owls and others were displayed in large glass cases. Subsequent shows had a mainly public service theme: one around 1930 featured a large working model of the Post Office tube railway. Model railway layouts were a 1930s Christmas feature, with realistic underground and above-ground stations. Natural gas was featured in 1931, whilst a display in 1938 used a vast pile of soot to emphasise the need for action to clean London's air. Post-war exhibits included jet aircraft (1946), the Women's Voluntary Service organisation (1947) the virtues of smokeless fuel (1953), holidays in Britain (1954) and electricity from nuclear energy (1955). Extensions of the Underground and other new tube facilities were the subject of regular exhibitions in this space, which was finally converted to retail units during the 1970s.

Mansion House is one of two stations with all five vowels in its name. The other is South Ealing. The Mansion House itself is in fact very close to Bank station, a few hundred yards down the road from the station that carries its name.

Mapping the tube. Not everybody carries a tube map in their head, which is why pocket maps of the network have existed almost as long as network itself. The first folding map of the Metropolitan Railway was produced in 1867, followed by more elaborate affairs with the lines superimposed on London street maps that were produced by the Metropolitan and District Railways. After 1900 these were joined by maps of the new electric tube railways, nearly all of which were set out on a more or less geographical basis.

The man who broke the mould was a draftsman named Harry Beck *(above)*, who boldly sketched out a completely diagrammatic map on which the location and spacing of stations owed little to physical geography. Beck enhanced this notion of user-friendliness with today's concept of 'tech-nology transfer', drawing on his familiarity with the rigid geometric layout and colour coding of electrical circuit diagrams. Beck's ideas were initially rejected but eventually accepted by the Publicity Department and the first pocket folder map was published in January 1933. The public took to this design immediately and Beck's concept has evolved to the present day with little fundamental alteration, copied by transport undertakings all over the world. It is now recognised as a design classic, even if Beck received scant recognition in his own lifetime.

March of Time. Time and timekeeping are vital to London Underground and to passengers, which is why great emphasis is placed on what is called service regulation, in other words ensuring that trains run according to the timetable. If not controlled properly, deviations from the timetable tend to be amplified by time, affecting the running of other trains and degrade the overall service quality. Service regulation of the line is used to maintain stable and timely train operation, also to avoid delays to passengers with consequential costs. Efficient and timely running also minimise inefficient energy consumption by using coasting and regenerative braking and helping to reduce tunnel temperatures. All of these measures assist London Underground to reduce transport's contribution to climate change.

Computerised intelligent train regulation systems being rolled out on the Underground play an essential part of meeting these objectives. By micro-managing train speeds and dwell time at stations, energy consumption is reduced up to 30 per cent and train crew scheduling is optimised.

Sophisticated techniques of this kind were unthinkable in the pre-computer era but the Underground was by no means helpless in the past. Already by the early 1930s ingenious methods were in use to regulate and record the running of trains. Many stations were equipped with one-handed headway clocks that must have puzzled many passengers. These clocks, installed next to where train drivers stopped at the front end of the platform, acted rather like stopwatches, being reset to zero each time a train departed. The pointer indicated how many minutes had elapsed since the previous train left — a time interval known as the headway — enabling the driver to judge whether he should leave immediately or wait a minute or two in order to maintain the timetable and 'regulate the service'.

This was not all that happened. Contact levers on the track next to the headway clocks were connected electrically to paper chart recorders installed at Underground headquarters at St James's Park station. As a train passed over one of these levers it caused a small inked hammer to strike the fringe of the circular chart, which itself rotated at the equivalent speed of a clock and as the hours went by, a succession of fine markings were printed around the periphery of the chart. A glance at the markings would tell whether trains were running with even spacing; gaps would appear if the trains were not running smoothly. Another of these recording clocks was displayed on the concourse of Piccadilly Circus station under the banner 'See How They Run'. This is no longer in place, but a clock showing world times *(below)* is.

Mile End station is unique in having cross-platform interchange below ground between Underground trains of the two different sizes used on the system. Here, the District Line large profile (or sub-surface) trains meet the Central Line tube trains on the same level, the Central Line being quite shallow at this point.

Mill Hill East station owes its existence to the siting of an army barracks opposite. When the Second World War began, a number of extensions to the Northern Line were in progress over existing steam lines. It was never the intention that this branch of the Northern should come to an end at Mill Hill East, but instead carry on to Mill Hill and Edgware over an existing alignment. For the benefit of those using the barracks, the line was extended to this point in May 1941 after all the other extensions started before the war had been suspended.

Mind the Gap. This familiar warning, given at stations with sharply curved platforms, is mentioned in instructions for platform staff dated 1923 and probably goes back earlier. Today it is played from recorded announcements. Various voices have been used over the years including that of the Archers actor Tim Bentinck who recorded 'Mind the Gap' and other safety announcements for a fee of £200 in 1990. Another actor, Oswald Laurence, had his voice restored to Embankment (Northern Line) in March 2013 following a request to TfL from his widow. The gap can be a foot or more, as can be seen at Bank (Central Line), Waterloo (Bakerloo Line) and Embankment (Northern Line northbound).

As the price of memory for storing the message has fallen, the modern digital announcers aboard trains are not constrained by cost considerations and these use the more meaningful phrase 'Please mind the gap between the train and the platform'.

'Mind The Gap' has become something of a catchphrase, appearing on souvenir tee-shirts and china coffee mugs and a plethora of books.

Missing from the map. Fictitious tube stations figure in many television programmes and movies. Some use elaborate sets created in the studio, whilst others shoot scenes 'out of hours' at actual stations that may be decorated to appear as other locations. The now closed stations Aldwych and Charing Cross (Jubilee Line) have substituted for many other stations and London Underground has a website that lists many of the feature films made at its stations (*http://www.tfl.gov.uk/tfl/corporate/media/lufilmoffice/*). The Waterloo & City Line, which has no service on Sundays, is another favourite filming location and was even more so in the past, when it belonged to British Rail and was available for use when London Transport was either unable or unwilling to provide facilities.

Mock-up stations have been created in studios since the inter-war years, not least the 1935 film *Bulldog Jack*, whose plot included a secret tunnel linking the British Museum to 'Bloomsbury' station (modelled on the former British Museum station closed in 1933).

A far more elaborate outdoor construction is the 'Walford East' station created on the back lot of the Elstree television studios where the BBC1 programme *EastEnders* is made. This fictional station has been placed on the map between West Ham and Bow Road on the District and Hammersmith & City Lines, replacing the actual station Bromley by Bow. Images of trains are inserted into programmes using computer-generated imagery (CGI), with audio effects added to the sound track in post-production. Further authenticity within the station interior is lent by ticket machines and barriers supplied by London Underground. Specially made timetables are made in the correct style and an example of these props can be seen at the National Media Museum, Bradford.

Perhaps the most sophisticated tube station effects yet achieved appear in the 2012 James Bond thriller *Skyfall*. These blend filming and virtual CGI imagery, the filming taking place at Pinewood studios and the disused Jubilee Line section of Charing Cross station. At Pinewood no fewer than 31 different sets were constructed on eight sound stages including platforms with the name Temple and the sewers beneath it. In a remarkable chase scene Bond chases the villain Silva into a station, where 007 pursues him sliding down an escalator, after which Silva leaps onto a train with Bond hanging to the back, ending in a dramatic crash. The scene filmed at Charing Cross involved replacing metal sections on the escalators with rubber replicas that bounce out of the way as our hero slides downwards.

More prosaic but extremely authentic, even in close-up shot, is the studio recreation of the fictitious Central Line station of 'Hobbs End' in the hinterland between Ladbroke Grove and Wormwood Scrubs. This was for the Hammer horror film *Quatermass and the Pit*, made in 1967, in which tunnel construction workers encounter a buried 'missile' that is not of this Earth. Amusingly 'Hobbs End' is also the name of one of the stations on a model railway used for training London Underground staff at Ashfield House, West Kensington. In the Hickory Dickory Dock episode of the television series 'Poirot', the internal scenes of Hickory Road station were filmed at Morden station with a preserved 1938 tube train.

Morgan, John P, is the man beaten by fellow American Charles Yerkes in his bids for building new tubes in the early part of the 20th century. He then went on to promote the building of the steamship *Titanic,* which he hoped would be more of a success.

Mornington Crescent — what a game!

Why should a relatively little-used tube station's name become a catchphrase? I'm sorry, I haven't a clue. But the Radio 4 comedy show of that name has certainly put this somewhat obscure location on the map. A regular element of the 'antidote to panel games' has been a session of the allegedly ancient parlour game of 'Mornington Crescent', in which players observe highly complex (but imaginary) rules. Opinions vary widely over the origin and creator of the game and the only undisputed fact is that the game was first broadcast on 22 August 1978.

The station itself closed for six years while it was being renovated and at its reopening on 27 April 1998, the regular cast of the show (the late Humphrey Lyttelton, Barry Cryer, Tim Brooke-Taylor and Graeme Garden) performed the ceremony. A memorial plaque to the late Willie Rushton, one of the longest-serving panellists, was installed at the station in 2002.

Moscow Metro and Gants Hill. Gants Hill station, opened in 1947, was one of the notable Tube architect Charles Holden's last three designs for the Underground and the magnificence of its platform level concourse, featuring a barrel-vaulted ceiling reminiscent of similar stations on the Moscow Metro, is indisputable. More questionable is the allegation made on several websites that Holden helped design Moscow stations, although it is established that Soviet engineers were impressed by Holden's work at Piccadilly Circus station and copied his uplighters. Whatever Holden's connections may have been, it is safe to say his design for Gants Hill was inspired by similar features on the Moscow Metro.

MORNINGTON CRESCENT
MORNINGTON · CRESCENT

WILLIE
RUSHTON
1937 - 1996
Satirist
COMIC HERITAGE

Mosquitoes. The mosquitoes that live in the tunnels of the London Underground are an example of evolution in action. Descended from mosquitoes that used to bite birds (*Culex pipiens*), and deprived of this food source, they have adapted to bite humans instead, and have lost the cold-intolerance that their ancestors had. Experiments by researchers at Queen Mary and Westfield College, London, showed that the mosquitoes are unable to breed with their original species, and they are now considered to be a separate subspecies and have been named *Culex molestus*. There are even genetic differences between the mosquitoes living on different lines.

Motormen and other American terminology. US financier Charles Tyson Yerkes, who controlled several of London's tube lines in the early years of the 20th century, brought with him not only capital but an entirely transatlantic approach to running railway. He imported a considerable quantity of rolling stock from the American Car & Foundry Company and the American railway jargon to go with this. Coaches or carriages were *cars*, bogies were *trucks* and train operators were *motormen*. Being gender-specific, the expression motorman is no longer used on London Underground but the other two terms remain in use.

Powered (end) coaches of electrical multiple units were and are *motor cars*, whilst intermediate coaches were and are *trailer cars* or *trailers*. Another American expression was the *gateman*, who operated the folding lattice gates at each end of the early tube carriages (sliding side doors were not fitted originally) and called out the names of the stations at each stop. The carriages themselves became referred to as 'cars', again after the American fashion. In the USA the terms *Eastbound* and *Westbound* took the place of what we call Up Line and Down Line. In 1905, when the District Line was electrified using American money and technology, these American terms were adopted (and retained, except for 'motorman' to the present day).

Multiple stations. Five London place names have four stations with their name: Acton (Acton Town, East Acton, North Acton, West Acton), Ealing (Ealing Broadway, Ealing Common, North Ealing, South Ealing), Finchley (Finchley Central, East Finchley, West Finchley, Finchley Road) and Kensington (High Street Kensington, South Kensington, West Kensington, Kensington Olympia). See also *Harrow and Ruislip* on page 37, each of which has five.

N

New Cross tunnel to nowhere. As part of the planning work for the Fleet (later Jubilee) line, an experimental length of running tunnel was constructed to the north of New Cross in 1972. This was on the then proposed alignment of the extended line, and so would become incorporated into the running tunnels when the third stage (from Fenchurch Street to Lewisham) was built. The 200-yard tunnel was used to trial a new type of tunnelling machine, which pumped a clay slurry called bentonite onto the working face of the tunnel to prevent unstable soil from collapsing during the work. The technique was successful, but the 1970s plans to extend the Fleet line were not, and hence the tunnel has remained as another abandoned relic.

The Next Station is... The electronic 'next station' indicators now standard on Underground trains are a boon to the hard of hearing and to anybody unfamiliar with the order of stations. But it will surprise the traveller of today that 'next station' indicators were already in use on District and Circle Line trains in the mid-1890s. Fitted above the seats in every compartment, there was nothing electrical about these indicators and they were in fact purely mechanical devices – worked by actuator arms mounted on sleepers. Unfortunately their operation was less than perfect and these ingenious devices were eventually considered too unreliable to be of use. They had another disadvantage — commercial sponsorship — as this contemporary description concedes: 'An attempt has been made to remedy this by fitting some trains with a device which, after ringing a bell, shows a plate bearing the name of the next station. But the greater part of each plate is occupied by an advertisement so that the provincial or foreigner might suppose the name of the next station to be Vinolia as easily as Aldgate'.

Night-time running. Historically the London Underground did not run around the clock, for two very practical reasons. The number of passengers who might be carried in the small hours was for most of its history so small as to make an all-night operation uneconomic. There is also the vital need to check, clean, maintain and repair stations, tracks and rolling stock, with the 'no wheels' period (correctly known as 'engineering hours') providing the only opportunity to carry out this important work. It is believed that the 1937 Coronation and the 2000 millennium celebrations were the only occasions when tube trains had run throughout the night until the introduction of regular weekend night services on some lines in 2016.

North Ealing is a particularly good surviving example of a District Railway station. The line between Ealing Common and Uxbridge was taken over from the District by the Piccadilly in 1932 and most of the stations were completely rebuilt, but North Ealing was almost untouched, save for a new substation being built next to the northbound platform.

Northern Line. Despite its name, the Northern Line has more stations south of the Thames than any other Underground line. It was named thus in 1937 to reflect its takeover of a number of north London steam services from the London & North Eastern Railway (once called the Great Northern). A 1990s plan to split the line into two, with a Stirling Line taking over the Bank and Barnet branches is on ice. Until 1988, when it was overtaken by one in Japan, the Northern Line had the longest continuous railway tunnel in the world, between East Finchley and Morden. It remains the longest on the Underground – at 17¼ miles.

Nothing but a façade deception at Leinster Gardens. When the Circle Line was constructed between Paddington and Bayswater in the late 1860s it was necessary to demolish two houses in a rather exclusive terrace of homes in Leinster Gardens, Bayswater. Leaving a gap between the remaining home would have created an eyesore and replicas of the missing houses were built to reinstate the symmetry of the view. However, the replacement homes were nothing more than facades that were just five feet deep. The illusion created by nos. 23 and 24 Leinster Gardens is remarkably convincing nonetheless and the dummy homes are complete with ornamental plants, railings and front doors (without letterboxes) and dustbins. The windows are, however, painted over now.

Most people are are totally unaware of this deception, which is why the addresses have played a part in countless practical jokes. It is said that back in the 1930s a joke was played on high society guests, who bought expensive tickets to a charity ball at this address. They discovered it was false only when they turned up there in evening dress and it is said that even today taxis and pizza deliveries are sent to 23 Leinster Gardens.

O

Oakwood station, one stop short of Cockfosters at the northern end of the Piccadilly Line, was in the middle of nowhere when it opened (some would say it still is). Being about half way between Barnet and Enfield – each about two miles distant –the original planned name for the station was East Barnet. It opened however as Enfield West, acquiring its current name in 1946.

One name, two stations. There are three names on the Underground that each apply to two completely separate stations: Edgware Road, Hammersmith and Paddington.

Out of station interchanges. To facilitate some journeys around the London rail network, interchanges that pass out of one station and back in through another are permitted. This is important for users of Oyster Pay-as-you-go, who would otherwise have to pay for multiple journeys. London Underground programs a list of permitted Out of Station Interchanges (OSIs) into the gatelines, which recognise such journeys and manage the fare appropriately. In some cases these permit interchanges that appear to be 'missing' from the network where lines cross but no interchange station is provided. These are: Bank ↔ Monument, Edgware Road (Circle and District) ↔ Edgware Road (Bakerloo), Euston ↔ Euston Square, Hammersmith (H&C) ↔ Hammersmith (District and Piccadilly), Hanger Lane ↔ Park Royal, Ickenham ↔ West Ruislip, Kenton ↔ Northwick Park, Paddington (H&C) ↔ Paddington (Circle and Bakerloo), White City ↔ Wood Lane.

Oxford Circus station, the fourth busiest station on the system, has two well preserved station frontages from the Edwardian era, one built for today's Central Line in 1900 on the east side of Argyle Street and one built on the west side for the Bakerloo Line in 1906. Both are today used as exits only from this busy station. It was a fire on one of the Victoria Line platforms here in 1984 that led to a ban on smoking on trains (a ban later extended to the whole system following the disastrous King's Cross fire in 1987).

Oval, which has a series of tiles in its booking hall showing cricketers, shares with Arsenal the distinction of being named after a sports ground, though until 1939 there was also a station on the Metropolitan Line at Lords. Oval is also one of only two stations on the Underground with a four letter name, the other being Bank.

No tube to Bromley – nor Bexley, Croydon, Kingston or Lewisham. These five south London boroughs have no tube stations within them.

Overseas outstations of the Underground. A small corner of London can be found in Berlin, in the busy district known as Schöneberg. On one of the platforms of Wittenbergplatz underground station is a sign donated by London Transport in 1952 to commemorate the 50th anniversary of the Berlin U-Bahn. This features the station's name in the distinctive round, red and blue style of signs on the London Underground.

A rather more substantial artefact exists in Disneyland Resort Paris, where Hayne Street 'Underground' station is one of the buildings that the studio tour bus passes. There are also numerous other appearances of the Underground roundel all over the world – often as signs for pub names or fashion shops.

P

Paddington Bishops Road was the original western terminus of the first underground railway in the world. Part of the original platforms are now served by Hammersmith & City Line trains and are an integral part of the main line station.

Parcels by tube. Around the corner from the main entrance of Farringdon Underground in Turnmill Street is a stone façade with carved lettering clearly saying 'Metropolitan Railway Parcels Office'. This is probably the last physical reminder what was once part of the Underground's business – carrying parcels. The Metropolitan ran a profitable parcels and newspaper delivery service, carrying 860,000 items of this kind a year in the mid-1920s, using 31 horse vans, two electric vans and 12 motor vans for collection and delivery. When use eventually declined the service was withdrawn at Circle Line stations (in 1936), while on the Aylesbury line the service was transferred to the LNER railway, which shared the route. Parcel services were also operated by the District Railway 'for the convenience of shoppers', the East London Line, the City and South London Railway (now part of the Northern Line) from 1891 to 1918 and the Central London Railway (Central Line) whose 'Lightning Parcels Service' ran from 1911 to 1917. These last two operations were hit by an acute manpower shortage towards the end of World War One. North of Harrow the service was run jointly by the main line railway and the Met before 1933 and it continued to be operated jointly after 1933. Newspapers continued to be carried on the Met Line until the late 1960s.

Park And Ride: hardly a novelty. When Morden station opened in 1926 the Underground provided covered shelter for cycles and nearly 500 cars, along with petrol pumps, workshop facilities and mechanics for servicing passengers' cars. It was the first of its kind in the country and far ahead of its time but not everybody considered it a welcome innovation. Parliament heard that whilst it appeared appropriate that people could leave their cars at the station and make use of public transport to get into the centre of the city, running garages was outside the Underground's remit and a threat to local small businesses.

Passenger emergency alarm

During the three years 2010/11 to 2012/13 there were a total of 4,862 passenger emergency alarm (PEA) activations. Of these, 2,662 were considered to be justified, with 2,020 activated maliciously, accidentally or spuriously.

Phantoms and fantasies. In its century and a half existence the London Underground has acquired a remarkably comprehensive mythology of ghost stories, few of which bear scrutiny (but still make a rattling good tale).

At Bank station it is said that that the Black Nun, named by some as Sarah Blackhead, still searches for her executed brother. The Paranormal Database states that a station worker once chased what he thought was an old lady locked in the station during the early hours of the morning, but she vanished down a corridor with no possible exit. In addition, at least one employee has reported something knocking on an empty lift door from the inside, way after the station entrance has been locked.

A tall man in a frock coat, top hat and gloves (the actor William Terriss) has been seen pacing the platforms at Covent Garden, whilst at Farringdon the cries of the Screaming Spectre (a 13 year-old girl called Annie Naylor murdered in 1758) are heard echoing down the platform. At Aldgate an old woman was seen by an engineer as she stroked his friend's hair, seconds before the co-worker touched a live high-tension cable (and survived). Phantom footsteps have been heard coming from down the tunnel and then ending abruptly.

The abandoned Central British Museum station on the Central Line is claimed to be haunted by a ghost of a long-dead Egyptian princess. Tales of a wailing spirit wearing just a loincloth and an Egyptian head dress are connected with the mummified member of Egyptian royalty, Amen-Ra, whose remains are stored at the museum. Apparently the wailing and screaming transferred to Holborn station after British Museum closed to passengers.

At West Brompton a man dressed in dark, old-fashioned workmen's clothing has been spotted early in the morning and late at night. He remains visible as he walks to the end of the platform, and then disappears. More ghoulish stories of the kind can be found by searching the Internet for 'Underground ghosts'.

Piccadilly Circus was the first Underground station to have fluorescent lighting, when in October 1945 the westbound Piccadilly Line platform was so fitted, the rest of the platforms at the station following soon after. Fluorescent lighting became common on the Underground from the 1960s.

Poems on the Underground. Public poetry can be cited as one of the success stories of the late 20th century, proving to be an excellent way of introducing the public to poetry. Launched in 1986 as Poems on the Underground, the concept has spread above ground to poems painted on the sides of buildings in several Dutch cities, then to Bulgaria and France. Credit for notion goes to American writer Judith Chernaik, who wished to bring poetry to a wider audience.

Poems, selected by Judith Chernaik, together with poets Cicely Herbert and Gerard Benson, are displayed on posters in 3,000 advertising spaces on the Underground. Financial support comes from Transport for London, the British Council, London Arts, the Poetry Society and the Arts Council. The programme aims to showcase a diverse range of poetry, including classical, contemporary, and international as well as work by up-and-coming poets. Proof of the pudding can be seen in the demand from passengers wishing to read more, which has led to the publication of a series of several books on this theme available in bookshops and from the London Transport Museum shop. The latter also sells copies of the poem posters.

Prime Ministers on the Tube. Prime ministers in recent times to have made trips in the tube have been Tony Blair, who travelled on the Jubilee Line to the Dome at North Greenwich in December 1999, and David Cameron on a trip from Epping to central London in April 2007. Both were accompanied by security staff and press photographers. In the early part of the 20th century it would not have been uncommon for prime ministers to use the Underground, though without the accompanying press and staff.

Q

Queensbury owes its name to the Underground. It was a name coined when the Underground was building a new station there, which opened in 1934. Prior to the station, there was little by way of housing development here and the area had no clear identity. Neighbouring Kingsbury, it was felt a very suitable choice for the budding suburb.

Queen's Park station has at its western end a Bakerloo Line depot that passenger trains travel through while in service, the only place where this happens on the whole system. Passengers unfamiliar with the arrangement here may well feel they have stayed on the train too long.

R

The Roundel – an iconic symbol of London. When the District and tube lines were rebranded *Underground* in 1908 a new symbol or emblem was introduced to identify station names more readily and the Underground name on publicity materials. This took the form of a horizontal bar superimposed on top of a solid red circle, identical to the Martini logo registered in 1929 and considered one of world's most recognisable trademarks.

Although the Martini company clearly considered this design desirable, it did not satisfy the Underground's publicity officer responsible for marketing, who became commercial manager in 1912. He saw (probably during the First World War) the bar and inverted triangle symbol of the Young Men's Christian Association (YMCA) that had been introduced in 1897 and asked his advisers for something of that quality, but more balanced. Edward Johnston, who had designed the Underground's own alphabet in 1916 (a modified form of which is still in use), provided the solution. He transformed the solid red 'bullseye' into a hollow ring, refining the emblem into a subtler, less cumbersome affair. This design was first employed for publicity purposes in 1919 and this iconic 'logo for London' remains in use today as the Roundel, a name given to it in 1971 when its proportions became fixed.

Several public transport operators around the world have adopted imitations of the design and in Britain both the LMS and Southern Railways employed bars and circles on station signs. Closer to home, the Metropolitan Railway, which had seen its *Underground* slogan purloined by its rival in 1908, felt obliged to improve station signing with a geometric symbol of its own. Wounded but not beaten, the Met decided to 'steal with pride' too. In 1914 it had adopted similar signs to its rivals but with a red diamond replacing the circle (a green diamond was used on the jointly owned East London Line).

Record breakers — the tube in a day. The first recorded attempt to travel the whole Tube network in just a day took place on 13 June 1959. Rules have evolved over the years and currently participants are required to visit all the stations on the London Underground network in the fastest time possible. Participants do not have to travel along every piece of track, only to pass through every one of the stations on the system, connecting between stations by using public transport or on foot. It did not take long for the 'Tube Challenge' to become recognised by the Guinness Book of Records and many attempts are made to support charities and other worthy causes. There is not and cannot be an all-time winner, simply because the number of stations on the network has changed over time. At the time of writing the official Guinness World Record stood at 15 hours, 45 minutes and 38 seconds (set on 21 May 2015 by Steve Wilson and Andi James) for 270 stations.

Royal Rider. Queen Elizabeth II visited the Underground five times. In 1939, as Princess Elizabeth she took her first journey on the Underground accompanied by sister Margaret and her governess Marion Crawford on 15 May. In 1969, the Queen performed the official opening of the new Victoria Line on 7 March. It was the first time that a reigning monarch had ridden on the Underground. The official opening ceremony took place at Victoria station, where The Queen unveiled a commemorative plaque on the station concourse and afterwards bought a ticket for five old pence to travel to Green Park. In 1977, Her Majesty rode at the front of a train on 16 December, when she opened the new Piccadilly Line extension to Heathrow Airport. In 2010, as recorded earlier in this book, the Queen visited Aldgate Underground station on 24 February, meeting station staff in the ticket hall and viewing a memorial plaque to victims of the July 7 bombings. In 2013 the Underground's 150th anniversary year, Her Majesty, Prince Philip and the Duchess of Cambridge visited Baker Street station and met staff there on 20 March.

S

Shortest-lived name ever given to an operational Underground station was Kennington Road, the present Lambeth North station, which opened with that name on 10 March 1906 and was renamed Westminster Bridge Road under five months later on 5th August that year. The name Westminster Bridge Road lasted for this station until April 1917.

Shortest names on the Underground are Bank and Oval.

St John's Wood is the nearest station to Abbey Road recording studios, where the Beatles recorded. The station houses the Abbey Road Café, selling not only refreshments but also Beatles' memorabilia.

St Paul's station, despite being in front of the cathedral, was named Post Office from its opening in 1900 until 1937. King Edward Building, part of the headquarters of the General Post Office, was situated behind the original Central London Railway station entrance, which was on the north side of Newgate Street. During the Second World War, the electricity grid control room for London and the South East was located in a disused lift shaft at the station.

Signalling, which has the task of ensuring the safe and efficient working of trains, is a function of all railway systems. On mass rapid transport systems, such as the London Underground, signalling has the additional task of maximising the potential of the railway to meet high levels of passenger demand in the rush hour by reducing the interval or 'headway' between trains. Traditionally this was achieved with visual signals observed by train operators (and complex supporting equipment), whereas nowadays many of the tasks of the train operator have been taken over by onboard computers, meaning that signalling is moving into an entirely new arena.

When the Underground opened in 1863 signalling was a far simpler affair. Traditional red signal arms mounted on wooden posts instructed train drivers to stop if horizontal or proceed with caution if inclined at 45 degrees. Signalmen communicated with each other by bell codes and telegraph needle indications. All of this paraphernalia differed little from the apparatus used on main line railways. With each decade that followed, distinctive signalling equipment, tailored to the special needs of underground railways was developed, such as colour light signals that used lamps only. Much of this followed American practice, for instance using compressed air rather than point rods or signal wires to activate the various devices.

Automatic control of trains became standard for new tube lines when the Victoria Line opened in 1968 as the first fully automatic passenger carrying railway in the world, along with train control offices supervising a complete line.

Smoke and smuts

How pleasant an experience was travel on the Underground when it was steam operated? Having stood on the platform at King's Cross when a steam train passed through the station (back in 1956) your author can state there was no discomfort at all but other opinions were ambivalent. The British author Henry Frith in his 1891 book *Triumphs of Modern Engineering* considered the problem solved:

> There are thirteen miles of the Inner Circle railway and in this distance occur more than double that number of stations. Some of these are more underground than others. But the ventilation was found to be very defective; complaints of the gas were heard from all stations; the glass was removed and the air permitted access. Some of the stations are planted in cuttings and plenty of ventilation is secured.

Newspaper reports of the offensive atmosphere of the London Underground were nevertheless numerous and they reached far beyond these shores. Benson Bobrick, in his 1981 book *Labyrinths of Iron*, quotes three undated reports in American publications which make dramatic reading.

> What is at first merely unpleasant soon becomes unhealthy and eventuates in a subtle poison, first affecting delicate organisations, and afterwards visiting alike the weak and the strong, the unhealthy and the healthy, engendering pestilence, and this is the ready ally of all contagious diseases. Surely such a calamity should not be visited upon any people under cover of an enactment for their benefit. [*Scientific American*]

> A coroner's jury has just condemned the atmosphere of the underground railway. The jury convened to look into the death at King's Cross Station, London, of a woman named Dobrier attributed her death to a bronchial ailment accelerated by "suffocating air. [*New York Post*]

Southfields station, in recent years, has had a makeover during Wimbledon tennis week, on some occasions having its platforms covered with Astroturf.

Southgate is the most northerly station on the Underground to be in tunnel. The Piccadilly Line emerges from tunnel between Bounds Green and Arnos Grove but then goes into tunnel again when it reaches the high ground of Southgate. The north tunnel mouth can be seen from the platforms. The station has a splendid 1930s circular station building, looking not unlike a flying saucer in a science fiction film.

South Harrow is an example of a name invented by the railway, which replaced a perfectly good name that already existed, the area it serves being known only as Roxeth until the railway arrived and its management wanted the station to be associated with the neighbouring town of Harrow. Today the name Roxeth has almost disappeared but lives on in the names of some local schools and a church.

Speaking in tongues. More than 300 languages are spoken in total in London, so it was welcome news when London Underground announced in 2009 that its ticket machines could now operate in 17 different languages. Up to then some of the touch-screen machines displayed instructions in six languages – English, French, German, Italian, Japanese and Spanish – but from 1 June of that year all machines in every station also had Arabic, Bengali, Chinese, Greek, Gujarati, Hindi, Urdu, Polish, Punjabi, Tamil, and Turkish. The upgrade, it was said, would give many people added confidence, help maintain London as a city that supports its cultural diversity and would also improve tourists' visits to the city. Posters in other languages are not new, however. The District Railway in east London issued posters and handbills in Yiddish in east London in 1907.

Spending a penny. There's a notion that toilet facilities are few and far between on the Underground but it's not strictly true. In fact around 75 Underground stations are so equipped, most being surface level stations on the outer parts of the system. In the central area only a handful of stations provide them and then only at the upper level. Most tube station platforms lie well below sewer pipes and the engineering cost of providing toilets at deep level would be very substantial.

Stained glass. Three Underground stations have stained glass visible to the passing passenger: Uxbridge, Hammersmith (H&C and Circle lines) and Barons Court. The stained glass at Uxbridge (*below*) is particularly impressive and incorporates the coats of arms of Uxbridge Urban District Council and the counties of Middlesex and neighbouring Buckinghamshire. The stained glass at Hammersmith is in the H&C ticket office area and that at Barons Court forms part of the station frontage.

Stamford Brook was the first Underground station to be equipped with automatic ticket gates. These came into operation on 5 January 1964. More recently, it established a book swap facility like many National Rail stations and a few other Underground stations. This one though got its own roundel and name: Stamazon Brook.

Stand on the right. Although road traffic in Britain overtakes on the right, the rule is reversed on escalators of the London Underground. Signs ask passengers to stand on the right-hand side, so that people in a rush can pass on the left. The reason for overtaking on the left is not arbitrary but a throw-back to the original 'shunt' or 'side-step' escalators, on which a diagonal barrier at the foot of the moving stairs meant the footway ended sooner for the right foot than for the left and forcing passengers to step off the moving stairway with their right foot in a sideways 'shunt'. Passengers who chose not to walk down the escalators were asked to stand on the right so that anyone wishing to overtake them at the end would be able to take advantage of the extra section of moving stairway. The so-called 'comb' escalators of today have no obstruction at the end of the moving staircase, with no technical reason to enforce standing on one side rather than the other. In 1921 a device called a Stentorphone was introduced at Charing Cross station (the present day Embankment) at the lower level of the escalators to the Hampstead Tube (today's Northern Line). This was a gramophone with a compressed air amplifier and was used to instruct passengers to stand on the right on the escalators.

T

Temple is the only station on the London Underground to share its name with a station on the Paris Metro.

Time to watch a film? Baker Street station, the one time gateway to Metroland and head office of the Metropolitan Railway, still has some of the air of a main line terminus station, including an elaborate war memorial on the eastbound Circle Line platform. Made of Carrara marble, this takes the form of an arch with Ionic columns supporting an allegorical statue of a lion overcoming a serpent. A naval shell from the First World War stands next to it, making an unusual charity collecting box. The other 'big station' trappings disappeared around the 1970s: a licensed bar, left luggage office, larger than normal bookstall – and a cinema. The 'Times' cinema had two entrances, one on the Station Approach in Marylebone Road and the other inside the ticket barrier on the station, enabling train passengers to delay their exit until the very last minute. The art critic Brian Sewell recalls that as a boy during the war of 1939-45, he was 'an addicted spender of pocket money in the News Cinema in Baker Street station'.

Titled trains. Names such as the *Brighton Belle*, *Orient Express* and *Flying Scotsman* evoke a sense of romance and 'specialness' that sets these trains apart from other, equally worthy services. Nowadays London Underground trains do not carry individual names (apart from a few special charter trains for enthusiasts) but this was not always the case. From January 1915 until 1932 'The Harrovian' provided a fast limited-stop service from South Harrow into central London along the District Line. Leaving at 08.13, it reached Mansion House station 42 minutes later, the fastest timing of the day. It managed this by missing out most intermediate stations, with only six stops between South Harrow and Sloane Square. The trains did not carry name boards.

Tolls on the Tube. Being charged just to use the passageways at a station may sound like a strange notion. Nevertheless, this seemed a reasonable means of recovering the substantial construction costs from people who were not actually travelling by train. A case in point was on the lengthy covered way that runs for a quarter of a mile beneath the streets from South Kensington station to the Science and Victoria and Albert museums. It was opened in 1885 by the Metropolitan District Railway company (the forerunner of today's District Line) so that passengers to reach the grounds of the newly opened Inventions Exhibition under cover. Nowadays it has exits into the Victoria and Albert, Natural History and Science Museums and is used by more than 50 million people every year.

Until 1908 a penny toll was charged to users who were not rail passengers (the remains of the booking office windows were still visible at each end of the subway until about 1970). An extension was planned to the Royal Albert Hall but was not constructed, although at one time there was a covered arcade to the Hall from where the present subway stops at the Science Museum. The subway is a Grade II listed structure, with its original finishes and architectural features largely intact. Unfortunately the subway is prone to leaking when it rains, sometimes to the extent that the subway has to be closed, ironically at the time when it's most useful. Tolls also used to be charged at Highgate station between Archway Road via the escalators to the Priory Gardens entrance.

Until much more recent times a fee was charged at Earl's Court station, which forms a very handy short cut (under cover) for people walking from the Earl's Court Road to Warwick Road. Both single and return tickets were sold. Southwark is another station that provides a handy short cut. The station's main entrance is at the corner of Blackfriars Road and The Cut but it also has entrances on the platforms of Waterloo East railway station, some way away, from which you can reach Waterloo Underground station. Interchange is permitted on one ticket as part of the same journey but people who are not making a rail journey must buy a platform ticket. A similar situation applies at the Bankside (south) entrance of Blackfriars station, where travellers can cross the river through the Network Rail station to reach the Circle and District Line station on the north bank. Others must buy a platform ticket. It is a curious fact that it costs £1, the price of an Underground platform ticket, to walk from Southwark to Waterloo East, but only 10p, the price of a National Railways platform ticket, to walk in the opposite direction.

Tottenham Court Road station received in 1986 what was almost certainly the most expensive London Underground platform décor ever when artist Eduardo Paolozzi designed and oversaw the application of an intricate pattern of mosaic tiles representing the local hi-fi industry. Much of this has since been removed in connection with the modernisation of the station as part of Elizabeth Line construction.

Tube. Although the expression 'Tube' is used almost universally to mean the London Underground, some people consider the word rather slangy. Originally the London deep tube companies adopted the term with gusto, erecting large illuminated 'TUBE' signs at stations. The word alliterated nicely in the nickname 'Tuppenny Tube' given to the Central Line when the same fare of two pence (2d) applied to any journey.

In 1908, the system was having second thoughts and announced to staff that it had been agreed: "to adopt the word 'UNDERGROUND' so that the Public may become accustomed to associate these Lines as a complete system of Underground Railways. A sign containing the word 'UNDERGROUND', as well as a large map of the 'Underground' System, to be illuminated at night, will shortly be placed on the outside of each Station. ... It is desirable that the use of the word 'TUBE' should now be discontinued.

Nowadays, reflecting public usage, Transport for London has no inhibition about referring to 'the Tube' in all publicity for the Underground.

Tubes for telecomms. The now-disused Royal Mail underground railway has already been mentioned (see Mail Rail) Another tube network under London belongs to BT (British Telecom) and is used for telecomms cables. The network of mainly 7-foot diameter steel-segment tunnels, built mostly during the four decades from the 1940s to the 1980s and runs for a total of around 12 miles, mainly in central London but with two spurs reaching out towards the north-western and south-western suburbs. From a constructional point of view there is much similarity between these cable tunnels and the tubes of the London Underground, with a number of connections at various locations between the two tube systems. During the Second World War telephone cables were also installed along several routes of London Underground tube tunnels to protect them from enemy bombing.

Also constructed underground was Kingsway trunk telephone exchange, built between 1950 and 1952 at Chancery Lane inside one of the wartime deep-level air raid shelters. Opened to traffic in 1954, Kingsway exchange played for three decades a major role in switching inland long-distance calls and later also became the London terminal of the first Transatlantic telephone cable, as well as the mid-point of the 'Hot Line' between the USA and the Soviet Union presidents during the Cold War.

As telephone exchanges go, the size of Kingsway was remarkable, with two parallel tunnels, each a quarter of a mile long and 16 feet wide, housing much of the equipment. Some three miles of racking were installed, carrying 337 miles of switchboard cable, along with a 1.5 megawatt generator for standby power generation. For all that, Kingsway telephone exchange is now vacant, superseded by newer technologies, while a new owner is found for this remarkable and once highly secret facility. London Underground has also installed third party telecoms cables in its tunnels and under-street ducts and it is a nice little earner.

U

Underground rivers on the Underground. Although most people imagine the Thames is the only river flowing through London, there are in fact several more that once flowed at ground level but are now enclosed in pipes or sewers below street level. Few of these lost waterways appear on normal maps or street plans, except when their names survive in street and neighbourhood names such as Fleet Street (a tidal inlet), Holborn (the hollow waterway) and Marylebone (church of St Mary next to the bourne or stream).

The best known of these is the Fleet River. It rises at Highgate Ponds and runs, via King's Cross and Farringdon Street, to the River Thames by Blackfriars Bridge. Although encased in sewer pipes, the water flow was sufficient to burst out in the Farringdon area at the time the Metropolitan Line was being built in 1862, causing major structural damage to the newly completed civil engineering works.

Another underground stream, fortunately less destructive than the Fleet, is the Westbourne, which flows from Hampstead through Kilburn, Hyde Park and Knightsbridge to enter the Thames at Chelsea. It is probably the most visible of London's underground rivers, simply because it passes over the platforms of Sloane Square station *(below)*.

Upminster Bridge. A so-called swastika motif is the centrepiece of the tiled floor in the circulating area at Upminster Bridge station. A degree of controversy (and misunderstanding) surrounds this feature, which some people appear to find surprising or insensitive, so it's worth examining in some detail. Constructed by the London Midland & Scottish Railway for District Line train services, the station dates from 1934. The station building is polygon-shaped, which is reflected in the design of its architectural details. For this reason the octagonal tile feature echoes a similar-shaped roof light above it and employs an equilateral cross with four arms bent at 90 degrees, an 'interesting' and perfectly symmetrical geometrical shape that is simple to construct with square tiles. The symbol is not actually a swastika (which is left-facing) but what is known in British heraldry as a *fylfot* or *gammadion*. True, the design had been appropriated in 1920 by the National Socialist (Nazi) party of Germany but it had not yet gained any connotations of fascist or racial ideologies at the time it was used at Upminster Bridge. The very same symbol was used in Britain during World War One on government savings stamps and as a decorative motif in several of Rudyard Kipling's books, so there was nothing questionable about using the device in the floor of Upminster Bridge station.

V

Ventilating the deep tubes. The deep tube lines have always had difficulties with heat build-up and stale air below ground. Three separate approaches have been taken to make the life of passengers more amenable. The first solution was to instal massive extraction fans above shafts dug between stations, although relief shafts were then required at the stations themselves as well to mitigate draughts. Keen eyes can spot these shafts; there is one south of Swiss Cottage station in Adelaide Road just east of Finchley Road, whilst another in Kennington Park was disguised as brick-built park shelter. Some are combined with electrical feeder stations that once served London's trolleybus system, such as one in Colina Road, just off the east side of Green Lanes. Another can be seen on the east side of Archway Road, just north of the Archway itself.

The second was to provide better cooling in station areas. The rising background temperature prompted trials in June 2006 of a cooling system at Victoria station, followed up in 2012 by the installation of air-chilling units *(right)* at Green Park and Oxford Circus stations. At Green Park wells were drilled to source naturally cool water for reducing the ambient temperature on the Victoria and Piccadilly Line platforms, whilst at Oxford Circus station air-cooling units are used in the ticket hall as well as on every platform.

The third approach was to provide cooling on board trains. Air-conditioned trains are now running on the Metropolitan Line and by 2016 the entire fleet of the 'sub surface' lines (Circle, District, Hammersmith & City and Metropolitan) will be air-conditioned. On the deeper tube lines the trains are a tight fit in the tunnels, leaving very little space for heat generated in the air cooling process to escape. Any heat removed from the train interiors would raise the temperature underground even more and hotter air would flood into the trains every time the doors were opened at stations. Rather than fight an unwinnable battle

against the laws of physics, London Underground and industry are banking on making the next generation of Tube trains lighter and more efficient, so that they generate less heat.

Victoria is the third busiest Underground station after Waterloo and King's Cross. A major building programme to expand capacity here was completed in August 2019 with the opening of a new northern ticket hall.

Vital statistics – 45% of the Underground is in tunnel. Each Underground train travels on average nearly 115,000 miles a year. The total number of passenger journeys each year is 1,107 million. The Underground has a total of 19,000 staff.

Victorian terrorism. A co-ordinated attack on the Circle Line by Irish-Americans occurred on 30 October 1883. The first explosion occurred at 8.05pm in the tunnel between Charing Cross and Westminster stations. Passengers awaiting trains at both stations were showered in broken glass and dust, whilst the explosion left a small crater 4 feet x 3 feet and 1 foot deep. Three minutes later another explosion took place in the tunnel 60 yards from Paddington (Circle Line) station, just as a train was passing. 60 passengers were injured, many seriously, cut by flying glass. Six train carriages were badly damaged and a hole was blown in the tunnel wall *(below)*. In January 1885, a bomb exploded on a Metropolitan Line train at Gower Street (now Euston Square) station. On 26 April 1897 a bomb left by an anarchist group on a Metropolitan Railway train exploded at Aldersgate Street station (now Barbican). Sixty people were injured, ten seriously, but the only fatality was a man who died from his injuries. A verdict of 'wilful murder' was recorded.

THE SPOT WHERE THE EXPLOSION TOOK PLACE, BETWEEN PRAED STREET AND EDGWARE ROAD STATIONS

In the 20th Century, Irish terrorism returned to the Underground in 1939 when bombs planted by the IRA exploded in the left luggage offices in the booking halls at Tottenham Court Road and Leicester Square stations on 3 February that year. Bombs were also left on the Underground by the IRA in 1973, 1976, 1991 and 1992.

W

War works — new roles for disused tube stations. During the Second World War several disused tube stations led new lives. Best known is Down Street, between Green Park and Hyde Park Corner stations, which was used as the protected headquarters of the Railway Executive Committee, a collaborative effort of the main line railway companies that co-ordinated train movements between the different systems. At extremely short notice arrangements had to be made for moving men, guns and ammunition from one part of the country to another. During the D-Day invasion period more than 70 ambulance trains were run each week. A section of the offices at Down Street was built specially for the use of Winston Churchill and the War Cabinet. Frequent use of this 'underground hive of industry' was made by Churchill and his ministers whenever necessary. Both Churchill and his wife used the place as alternative sleeping quarters from 1941 to 1943. During the bombing Mrs Churchill would sometimes emerge onto the platform and travel by tube train to various stations to make surprise visits to people sheltering on the platforms.

At nearby Green Park station an area was fitted out as an emergency bolt-hole for the chairman of London Transport and two dozen of his departmental heads. Other emergency offices were built on the disused Aldwych branch platform at Holborn for the operating managers and their staffs. British Museum station on the Central Line (closed in 1933 when it was replaced by Holborn Kingsway) was reopened in 1941 as a public air raid shelter, whilst Brompton Road on the Piccadilly line was used throughout the war controlling the anti-aircraft guns defending London.

Disused areas of Aldwych, Green Park, Piccadilly Circus stations were used for safe storage of the Elgin Marbles, precious paintings and valuables of the London Museum. At Earl's Court a small factory was established in a disused subway for making aircraft components.

Water ingress whether from flooding or underground springs or watercourses is a serious problem for London Underground. The problem is aggravated by ground water levels, which have been rising in London by as much as 3.5 metres a year since the 1960s, following the demise of industries such as brewing and paper production that previously extracted large volumes of water. London Underground has to deal with regular flooding in parts of its network and has to pump more than 47 million litres of water from the system every day, using a total of 1,125 pumps at 714 different locations. Inundation of the system is not the only problem facing the Underground; resaturation of the London Clay through which tube tunnels pass is likely to prove more problematic because it will reduce bearing capacity and could increase subsidence.

Waterloo. During the three-hour morning peak, Waterloo is London's busiest Tube station, with almost 30,000 people entering. The busiest station in terms of passengers each year is also Waterloo with 41 million users. It has interchange between four tube lines and busy main line commuter services. It is one of only two Underground stations with moving walkways (the other being Bank) and is the station with the most escalators (23).

Waterloo & City line – sold for £1. As well as being the shortest line on the Underground (2.4 km), and the line with the fewest stations (two), the Waterloo & City has the distinction of being the newest line owned by London Underground. It was originally backed by the LSWR, which then acquired it; as such, it eventually became part of British Rail. It was sold to London Underground for a nominal £1 with ownership transferring on 1 April 1994.

West Ashfield station is equipped with a passenger entrance, ticket office, a standard gate barrier line and the other accoutrements of a normal station. What makes it unusual is that the whole affair is situated on the third floor of an office block, Ashfield House in West Kensington. It is in fact "a fully fitted out fake tube station built by London Underground and is used to teach new employees what goes where and when", says blogger Ian Mansfield.

Opened in 2010 at a cost of £800,000, this highly realistic simulation is so real that it is equipped with a platform, fitted out with real station fittings in full size but significantly shorter than a real station. There are no moving trains, however, only a replica end profile of one, which is rather handy as the 'suicide' prevention pit between the rails is no more than a painted effect. The overall effect is nevertheless quite convincing, with a fan simulating the familiar blast of air when a train arrives and equipment for simulating the rumbling of an approaching train. Other facilities in the training centre include a computerised driving simulator in the cab of an S stock train, also full-sized signals and trackwork for demonstration and skill training purposes.

The station's name, West Ashfield is in honour of Lord Ashfield, who followed a distinguished career on the Underground from 1910 to 1947.

West Hampstead has three separate railway stations with the same name. 100 metres north of the Underground station is the London Overground station and 100 metres north of that is the Thameslink station. Earlier in the 21st century there were proposals to link all three with a major new mixed-use development, but nothing has come of this so far.

Westminster station was the site of a complicated engineering feat in the 1990s when the Jubilee Line was being extended. The proximity of the works to the Big Ben tower required constant monitoring of its foundations – monitoring which continues today – with strengthening of the tower's foundations as necessary. The station is extremely convenient for the Houses of Parliament. For many years it has had an exit direct from the station under Bridge Street reserved for Members of Parliament and other pass holders. Until the station was rebuilt to accommodate the Jubilee Line platforms (opened in 1999) the passageway to the Houses of Parliament ran directly from the station's sub-surface circulating area. Since then access has been not from the station itself but via a clearly marked stainless steel doorway next to the subway that runs under the road.

White City station has received two architectural certificates of merit in its time. Built in 1947, it received an award in the 1951 Festival of Britain (a plaque commemorating this appears to the left of the entrance) and in 2009 it received a certificate of merit in the National Railway Heritage Awards.

Whitechapel is served by both London Overground and London Underground. Nothing uncommon about this, but the station is unique in that the London Overground service here passes under the Underground. At places other than stations, the Underground also goes over the Overground at Chiswick Park, Kenton, and West Hampstead.

Women workers were first employed on all lines of the Underground during the First World War starting in 1915, as 'wartime substitutes' when the number of employees conscripted into the forces made for severe staff shortages. Roles considered suitable for female workers included ticket collectors, lift attendants and porters. From 1917 they were also employed as station guards, guards and 'gatewomen' on trains who opened and closed the gates at the end of each coach (before sliding doors were introduced).

It cannot be denied that some prejudice existed against the employment of women for railway work but this was by no means universal. Researcher David Welsh records that Lord Aberconway, chairman of the Metropolitan Railway, argued 'lady' ticket collectors did better than their male counterparts. Passengers appreciated them too; one female ticket collector on the Central London Railway was observed by the *Railway Review* 'perched on the examiner's box, with legs crossed, and her uniform hat at a rakish angle'. Other roles taken up by women included acting as guards on electric trains, cleaning trains, painting and bill-posting. Subsequently women took on many other tasks, one of the more unusual being removing all the fluff and other detritus that accumulated in tube tunnels. This job was done in the middle of the night, when no trains were running, and the 'fluffers' (as they are known) were celebrated in a number of cinema newsreel films. It was not until 1978 that the Underground appointed its first female train driver.

World Time Clock. A unique feature, dating from the late 1920s is the World Time Clock at Piccadilly Circus. Built into the inner wall of the circular concourse, this unusual timepiece is a linear clock with a slowly moving band marked out in hours that moves across a map of the world. An arrow fixed on Greenwich shows the current time in London but you can also see the approximate time anywhere else around the globe. The arrow is moveable to allow for summer time adjustment. See photo on page 50.

X

X marks the spot of entry into the labyrinth designs that began to appear at London Underground stations in March 2013. Contemporary artist Mark Wallinger was commissioned to create a major new artwork to celebrate the Underground's 150th anniversary. His idea was to have a labyrinth wall panel at each of the 270 stations on the system. Produced by the same method as the Underground's station name signs, using vitreous enamel, each labyrinth is numbered in the order of stations visited by the current holders of the record for visiting all of the stations in the shortest possible time (see *Shortest time* entry)

Y

York Road station near King's Cross, closed in 1932, still stands and clearly displays its name eighty years later for curious passers-by to see. It was a station on the Piccadilly Line between King's Cross and Caledonian Road.

Z

Zero point. All distances on the Underground are measured from a notional zero point at the buffer stops at Ongar station. Ongar was closed on 30 September 1994, but the cost and effort of replacing all of the measurement plates (typically one every 200 m) is such that the zero point remains some 9.8 km away from the nearest Underground station at Epping.

Zones. For many decades public transport operators charged fares on a distance-travelled basis, which had the advantage of fairness but, in London at least, the disadvantage of major complications in fare collection, ticketing and accounting. To simplify fares and fare collection many cities around the world use the fare zone system, with flat fares within each zone. This simplifies charging for operators, whilst passengers know in advance exactly how much their journey will cost. Drawbacks are few, the greatest from a passenger perspective being that shorter journeys become more expensive, particularly if the journey crosses a zonal boundary.

In London fare zones arrived relatively late, on account of the large geographical area covered and the need to embrace a complex network of bus, Underground and suburban rail services run by a number of separate operators. Zones were finally introduced – and modified – during the years 1981 to 1991. Fares were indeed simplified, ticket issuing speeded up and Travelcards introduced.

There are now six main zones, corresponding approximately to the Greater London boundary, with three additional zones outside Greater London where fares are set by Transport for London. These zones (7, 8 and 9, formerly A, B, C and D) extend into Buckinghamshire and Hertfordshire; these do not encircle London in the way that lower-numbered zones do. These zones apply only to journeys on Metropolitan Line and Chiltern Line trains. B, C, G and W are additional zonal areas, not shown on maps, that are used for pricing certain Oyster Card pay-as-you-go journeys on National Rail services in Essex and Hertfordshire.

Generally the zone system works well, because the most popular destinations and the stations where lines cross are in zone 1, meaning that most journeys over similar distances will cost the same. The greater distance between stations in outer areas means that some zones contain only one or a couple of stations. Just one section of the Underground has a two-zone jump between stations – the Metropolitan Line between Finchley Road (zone 2) and Wembley Park (zone 4). Some stations are located on the boundary of two zones, meaning that passengers need to purchase only a ticket covering the zone(s) they require.

Bibliography

Badsey-Ellis, A., *Constructing London's Underground* (Capital Transport, 2016)
Badsey-Ellis, A., *Underground Heritage* (Capital Transport 2012)
Badsey-Ellis, A., *The Birth of the Tubes* (Capital Transport, 2019)
Badsey-Ellis, A., *The Hampstead Tube* (Capital Transport 2007)
Barker, T.C., and Robbins, M., *A History of London Transport Vols 1 & 2* (Allen & Unwin 1963/1974)
Bayman, R. E., *Underground Official Handbook* (Capital Transport 2008)
Bownes, D., Green, O., and Mullins, S., *Underground: How the Tube shaped London* (Allen Lane 2012)
Brown, J., *London Railway Atlas* (Ian Allan 2006)
Chernaik, J. (Ed.), *Poems on the Underground: A New Edition* (Penguin 2012)
Connor, J. E., *London's Disused Underground Stations* (Capital Transport 2012)
Croome, D.F., and Jackson, A.A., *Rails Through the Clay* (Capital Transport 1993)
Day, J. R., and Reed, J., *The Story of London's Underground* (Capital Transport 2019)
Emmerson, A., and Beard, T., *London's Secret Tubes* (Capital Transport 2004)
Emmerson, A., *Underground and Overground Trains* (Capital Transport 2013)
Garland, K., *Mr Beck's Underground Map* (Capital Transport 1994)
Glover, J., *London's Underground*, 12th edition (Crecy, 2015)
Glover, J., *Principles of London Underground Operations* (Ian Allan 2000)
Green, O., *London's Underground*, (Frances Lincoln, 2019)
Gregg, J., *The Shelter of the Tubes* (Capital Transport 2001)
Halliday, S., *Underground to Everywhere* (Sutton Publishing 2001)

Harris, C.M., *What's in a Name?* (Capital History 2005)
Horne, M.A.C., *London's District Railway Volume 1 The Nineteenth Century* (Capital Transport, 2018)
Horne, M.A.C., *London's District Railway Volume 2 The Twentieth Century* (Capital Transport, 2019)
Horne, M.A.C., *The Piccadilly Tube* (Capital Transport 2007)
Jackson, A.A., *London's Metropolitan Railway* (David & Charles 1986)
Jackson, A.A., *London's Metroland* (Capital History 2006)
Lawrence, D., *Bright Underground Spaces* (Capital Transport 2008)
Lawrence, D., *A Logo for London* (Capital Transport 2000)
Leboff, D., *London Underground Station Encyclopaedia* (Capital Transport, 2024)
Leboff, D., *London Underground Stations* (Ian Allan 1994)
Long, D., *The Little Book of the London Underground* (History Press 2009)
Marshall, Geoff, *Tube Station Trivia* (Capital History 2018)
Ovenden, M., *London Underground by Design* (Penguin 2012)
Ovenden, M., *Away From it All By Underground* (Capital Transport 2020)
Roberts, M.J., *Underground Maps After Beck* (Capital Transport 2005)
Roberts, M.J., *Tube Map Travels* (Capital Transport 2019)
Stanway, L.C., *Mails Under London* (Assoc. Essex Philatelic Societies 2000)
Taylor, S. (Ed.), *The Moving Metropolis* (Lawrence King 2001)
Wolmar, C., *The Subterranean Railway* (Atlantic 2004)

Websites

Transport for London: www.tfl.gov.uk
London Reconnections: www.londonreconnections.com
Underground History: underground-history.co.uk